NIAGARA

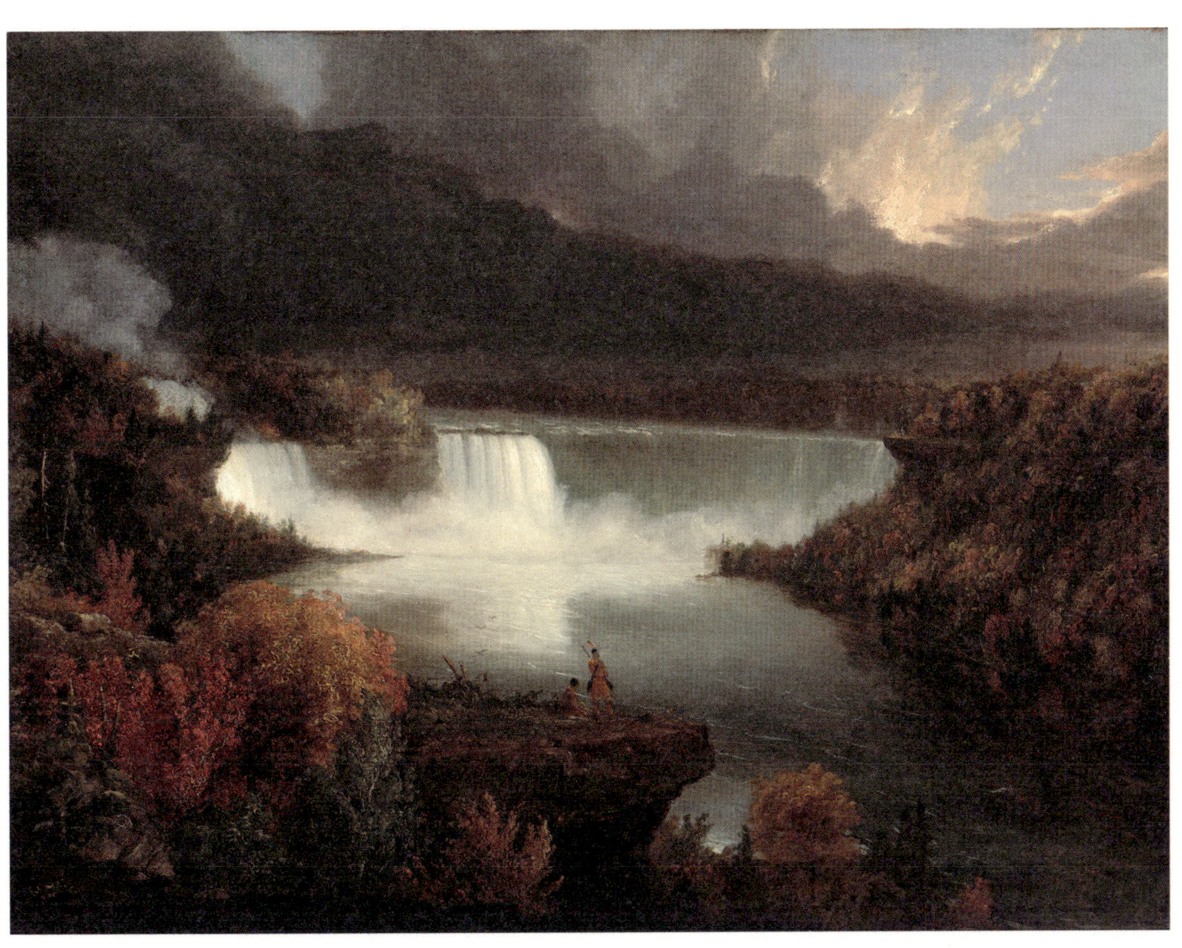

In the 1830s, the area around Niagara Falls was still mostly wilderness. Railroads were just coming in, and already people were complaining about how commercialization was ruining Niagara Falls. Already there were cheesy attempts to make money off tourism. In 1827, promoters sent a ship full of animals over the falls. They had advertised that it would be ferocious animals of the forest—panthers, wildcats, wolves; instead, the cargo included a buffalo, two foxes, a raccoon, a dog, and 15 geese. It didn't matter. Everybody made money. The town of Niagara Falls had barely been settled for two decades.

This kind of exploitation of the falls has continued for nearly two centuries since then. And what's surprising about it, really, is how unsuccessful it's been. Power plants fell into the river. Bridges collapsed. Deals were struck that benefited no one. If the classic story of America is the story of people who started with nothing, pulled themselves up by their bootstraps, made something of themselves, the story of Niagara Falls is the opposite story. Here, they started with something—something big, something huge— but didn't build anything lasting from it.

The modern history of Niagara Falls can be divided roughly into three phases—the schemers who came in trying to exploit the falls for tourism, how their dreams rose and fell. But that's not the story we're here to tell today. Then there were the schemers who came in trying to exploit the falls for industry. By the twentieth century, they built hydroelectric power plants and factories that used that power—that cheap power— moved in. But then those factories left, decimated by the same economic forces that ravaged the industries in most of the Rust Belt states, forces so powerful they can destroy a town, even a town with one of the world's natural wonders in it.

But that's not the story we're here to tell today, either. We're here to tell the story of the third phase of Niagara's life: the people who live in the aftermath of those dreams that have been dreamt and lost, who live in present-day Niagara Falls, a city—like many cities around the country—blessed at some point with natural advantages and resources that somehow fell from grace, fell apart; a town full of people trying to make sense of what's happened, living in the aftermath of what's happened, some who've made their peace with what Niagara is, some who haven't.

During the next half hour, we're going to bring you two sets of stories interlaced, half of them from documentary producer Alix Spiegel, who went to the falls and interviewed people living there, half from David Kodeski, who grew up in the town of Niagara Falls. It's *This American Life*, from WBEZ Chicago, Public Radio International. I'm Ira Glass.

Stay with us.

IRA GLASS

All the stories this hour will be from Alix and David. We'll start with this one from Alix.

ALIX SPIEGEL

There's a painting of Niagara above the couch in Paul's living room and another on the opposite wall over a chair. These pictures have a romantic, epic feel, like the two Niagara pictures he's hung on the wall near the front door. Then there are the four aerial photographs of the falls above the greenhouse window and the etchings of the falls in his office and the small, delicate portrait of the falls in the kitchen over the sink. There is, in fact, a picture of Niagara on almost every wall of every room in Paul's house. I visit Paul, and we sit together on the couch in his living room under the biggest picture of blue water rushing the brink.

He's wearing his Niagara baseball cap.

PAUL GROMOSIAK

Walking toward the falls you can notice the crescendo building up, the change. Then you can hear this *mmmmmm* and that sound of the falls as you're getting closer and closer and closer. And finally you're there. It's like the *1812 Overture*, when the symbols go *boom! Dum-da-da-dum!* I get goosebumps when I hear that, every time I hear it. Honest to God. If you've ever heard the *1812 Overture*, I'm sure—well, that's the same feeling. That's what people should get when they go to Niagara— goosebumps.

ALIX SPIEGEL

Paul was a schoolteacher but retired early so he could study and write about Niagara full-time. He's written five books, a folder of poems and gives lectures to local high schools and environmental groups. Nothing about the falls is too small for Paul to study; he is, for example, the only person ever to compile a comprehensive history of suicides at the falls. He did this by combing through a century's worth of newspapers at the local library, picking out all the articles and references to suicide, and collecting this information in a series of graphs—colored bar charts on poster board—that break the suicides down by age, sex, and so on.

PAUL GROMOSIAK

Monday, blue Monday, I guess is the most popular day. Wednesday is the least popular. Over the hump. People always feel good. Over the hump. Weekend's coming, so who wants to do away with themselves? We got the weekend coming. And then what time of the day are suicides? 4 o'clock in the afternoon. So tired of work. Can't stand it. Can't decide to go home or whatever. And then what month of the year? September is the most. And, believe it or not, the next month is the least: October.

ALIX SPIEGEL

Paul reads me a poem he wrote, called "Sensing the Wonders of Niagara." He tells me that the American Falls and the area around the American Falls is supposed to be a natural reserve, according to a hundred years of New York state law. But, he says, the city of Niagara doesn't care. He says there are too many skyscrapers, too much honky-tonk, too many factories, and tourist helicopters buzzing low all day long. On the Canadian side of the falls, there's casino gambling and wax museums and sushi.

Then Paul starts asking me questions—not the kind I'm supposed to answer, the kind that answer themselves. Who are we, the residents on either side of this wonder, to think that it is ours to do with as we wish? Why do we insist on introducing more and more buildings and distractions around the falls? Why must we turn the falls into a commodity? How come so many people are so unhappy today? Why are people angry when they drive? Isn't this because there are no places of natural beauty where people can escape modern life?

PAUL GROMOSIAK

How would it look if you stood in line at the Louvre in Paris to see the *Mona Lisa*, as I did in 1979—how would it be if, when you finally got

to see it, there were neon lights all around it, flashing. Buy this. Buy
that. Buy this. Could you really enjoy the painting? No. If you went to
hear Mozart—oh, my favorite composer, Mozart. If you wanted to hear
Mozart and went to a concert, and you've waited for months to hear this
concert, and then, right next to the stage was a rock band playing at the
same time—could you enjoy the Mozart? I'm afraid not. So when you
come to see Niagara Falls, you should see something natural. When you
come to hear Niagara Falls, you should hear something natural.

ALIX SPIEGEL

Paul writes letters to the *Niagara Gazette* and the *Buffalo News*,
and speaks out at town meetings about limiting commercialization
of the area around the falls. His opinions are unpopular. He's seen
as an outsider, an extremist. He's been called a complainer and
anti-industry. One city councilman told one of his friends that he'd like
to see Paul disappear. In 1983, Paul was testifying against a landfill that
he thought might threaten the Niagara River. And that night he was
woken up at three in the morning by the sound of a truck in his driveway.

PAUL GROMOSIAK

A truck pulled up in my driveway and put a large metal sawhorse against
my overhead garage door. And my dog was barking. I got up and I just
got to see the truck leaving my driveway. And there were two men on the
back of the pickup truck and a man driving. And there were two blinking
amber lights on the sawhorse. I put my coat on, went outside, and I took
a look at it. I said, my god, why is this here? So I called the police. And
the sheriff came to my house. And he said Mr. Gromosiak, you've been
warned. I said, by whom? He said, I don't know, but that's how they
warn people. I said, oh, really?

ALIX SPIEGEL

As a kid, Paul would visit Niagara three or four times a week. He would
sit on his favorite stump, watch the water, and fantasize about what his
life would be like. But now Paul doesn't visit Niagara at all. He lives less
than three miles from the falls, studies and writes about the falls every
day, covers his walls with pictures of the falls, but he can't bring himself
to go.

PAUL GROMOSIAK

For relaxation, I can't anymore. I just can't. I get upset now. I could cry. I feel like I'm walking on the ruins of a wonder. So I go other places to walk.

ALIX SPIEGEL

When you think about your life in the future, do you ever think that you will be able to—

PAUL GROMOSIAK

No. No. No, I can't. I don't think I will. I will only go there when I have to, to do a favor for someone or to take people there to see it. But I will remind them about what it was.

ALIX SPIEGEL

Paul tells me that he sometimes thinks that fighting for the falls is his destiny. He never married and lives alone, so he has plenty of time to really pursue it. And, ultimately, he believes he will see a natural Niagara Falls, one day, when he gets to heaven.

PAUL GROMOSIAK

Could you imagine being in that place forever, how it used to be, with the bald eagle soaring above, hundreds of them, with that ground shaking, with the trees bending over the gorge, growing larger than most other places in North America, all kinds of food to eat? Just cup your hands together and put them in the water and drink it while you're looking at the falls. I can deal with that forever. I can deal with that forever.

break

CITY & REGION

Elmwood Avenue Festival of the Arts

Shooting leads to ... purchase; 3 arrested

A few tips for incoming freshmen

A movable feast for local rats

Color didn't matter in our zone

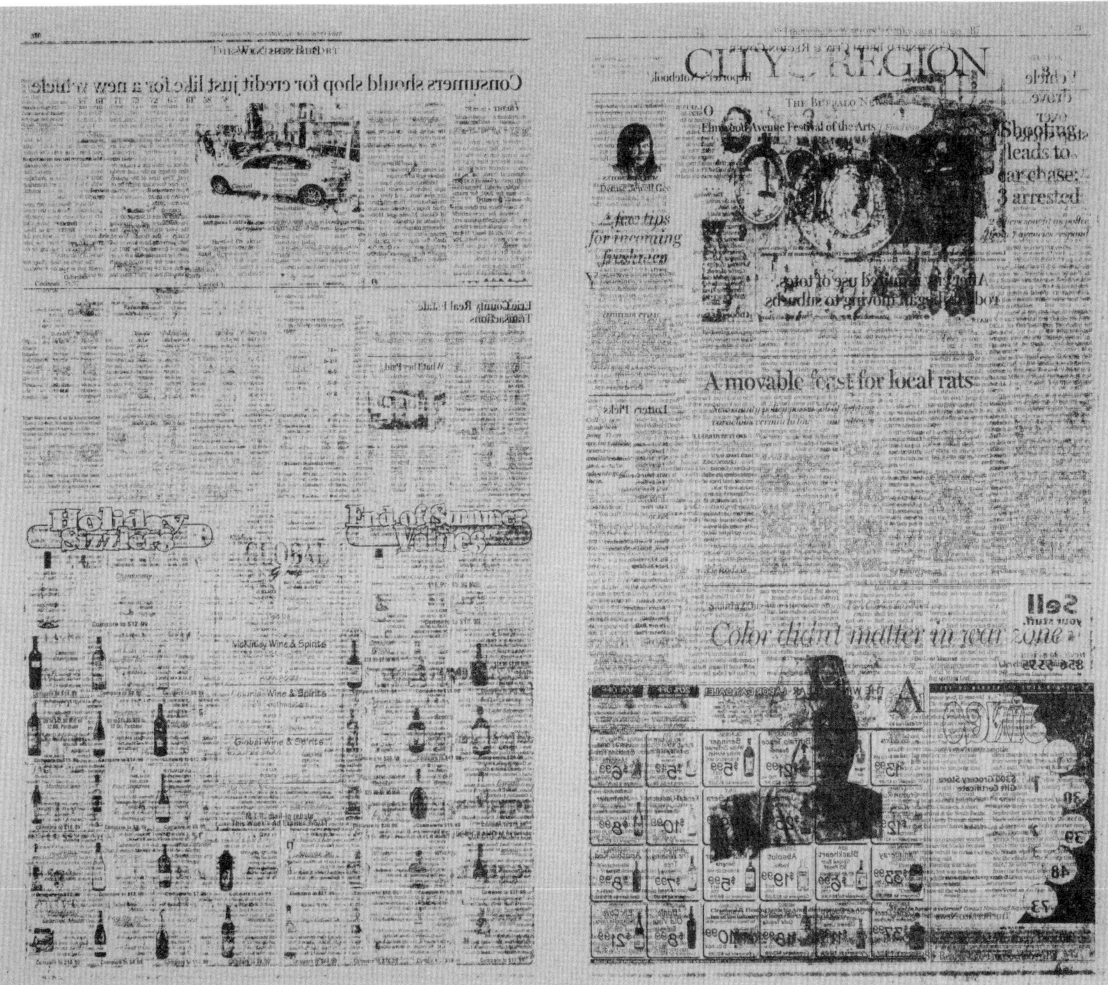

Consumers should shop for credit just like for a new vehicle

Holiday Sizzlers

End of Summer Values

GLOBAL

McKinley Wine & Spirits

Colonial Wine & Spirits

Global Wine & Spirits

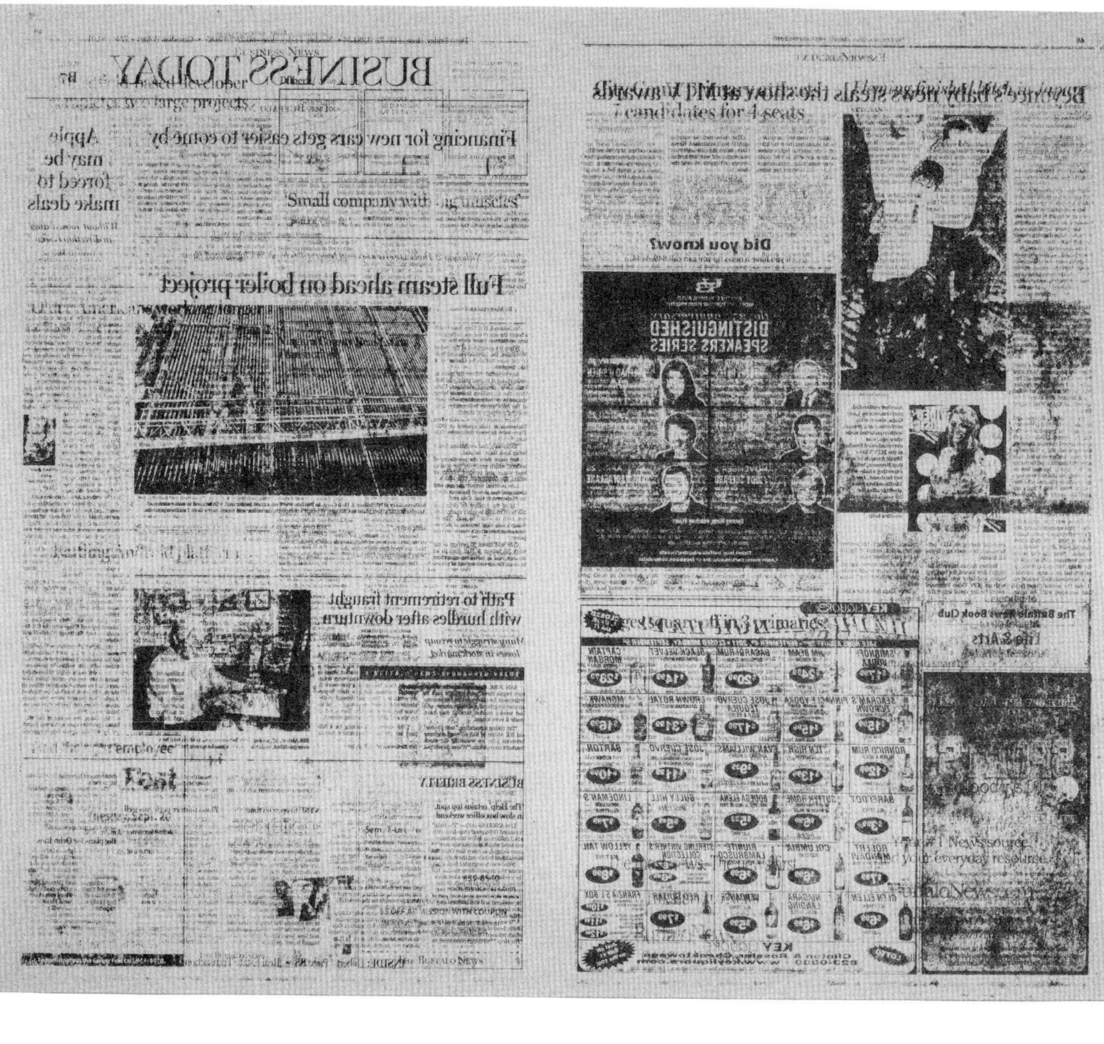

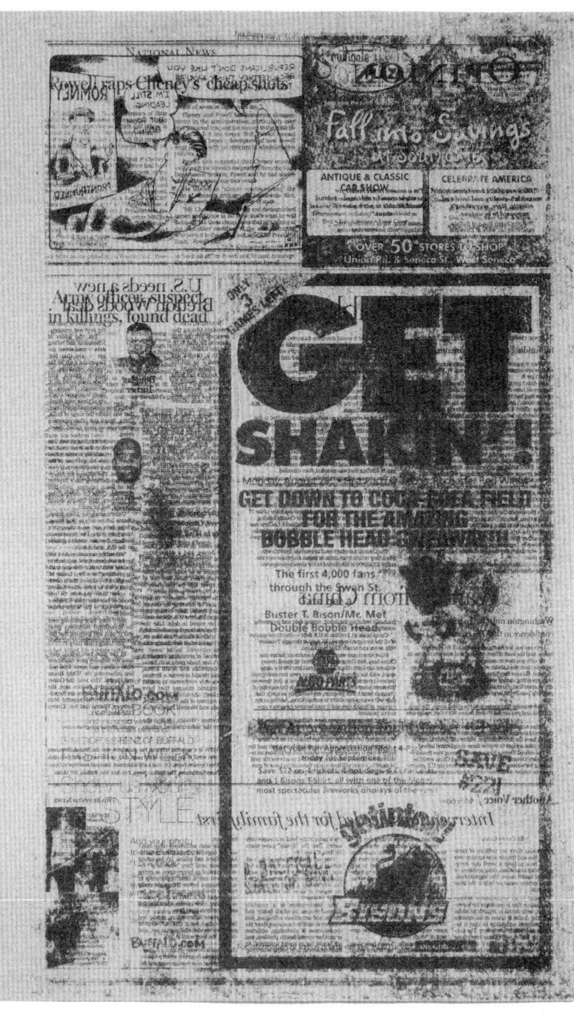

ONLY 3 GAMES LEFT
GET SHAKIN'!
GET DOWN TO COCA-COLA FIELD
FOR THE AMAZING
BOBBLE HEAD GIVEAWAY!
The first 4,000 fans
through the Swan St.
Buster T. Bison/Mr. Met
Double Bobble Head
AUTO PARTS
Family Fun Appreciation Night 4-Pack
today
Save $22 on 4 tickets, 4 hot dogs
and 1 Bisons T-Shirt, all with one of the biggest
most spectacular fireworks displays of the year!
SAVE $22
BISONS

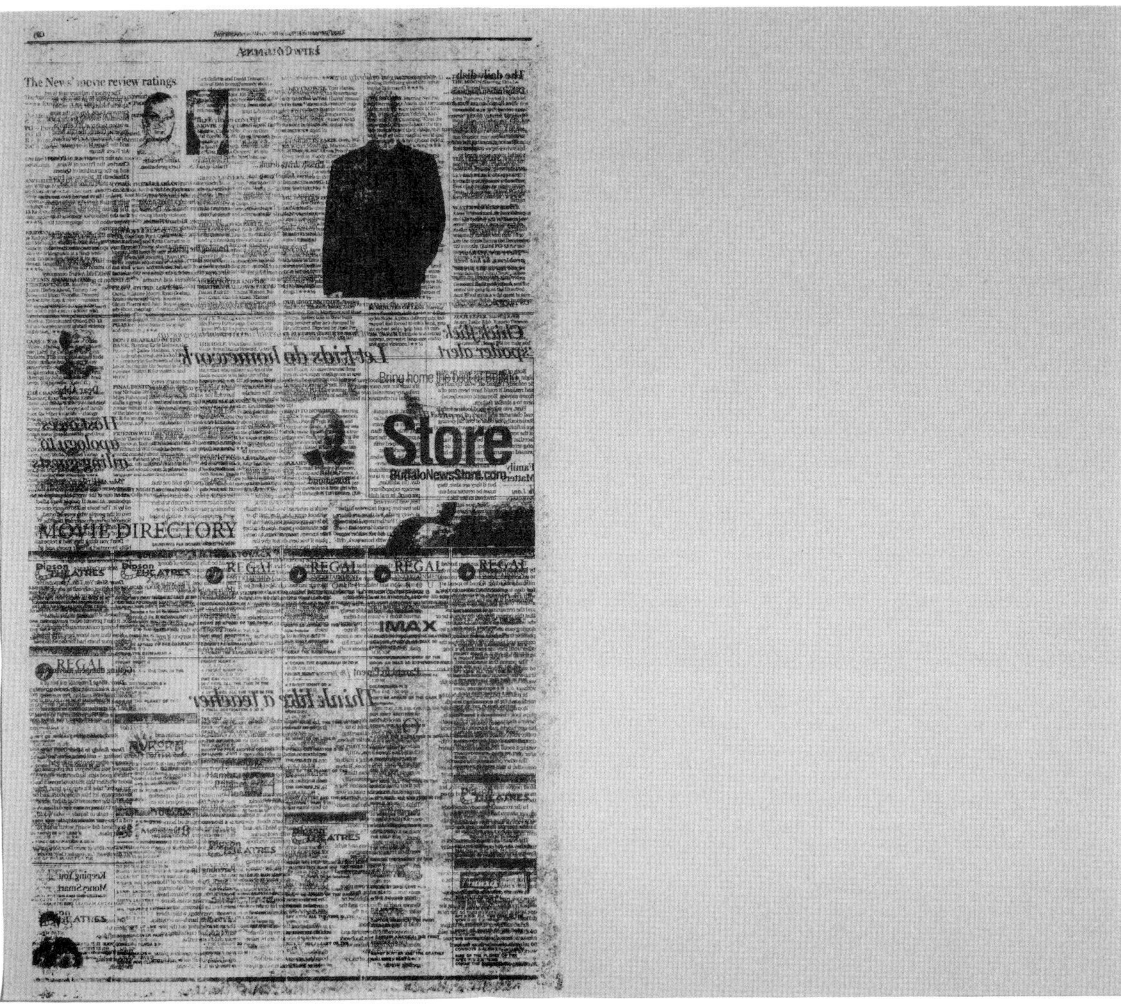
The News' movie review ratings
Store
BuffaloNewsStore.com
MOVIE DIRECTORY
IMAX

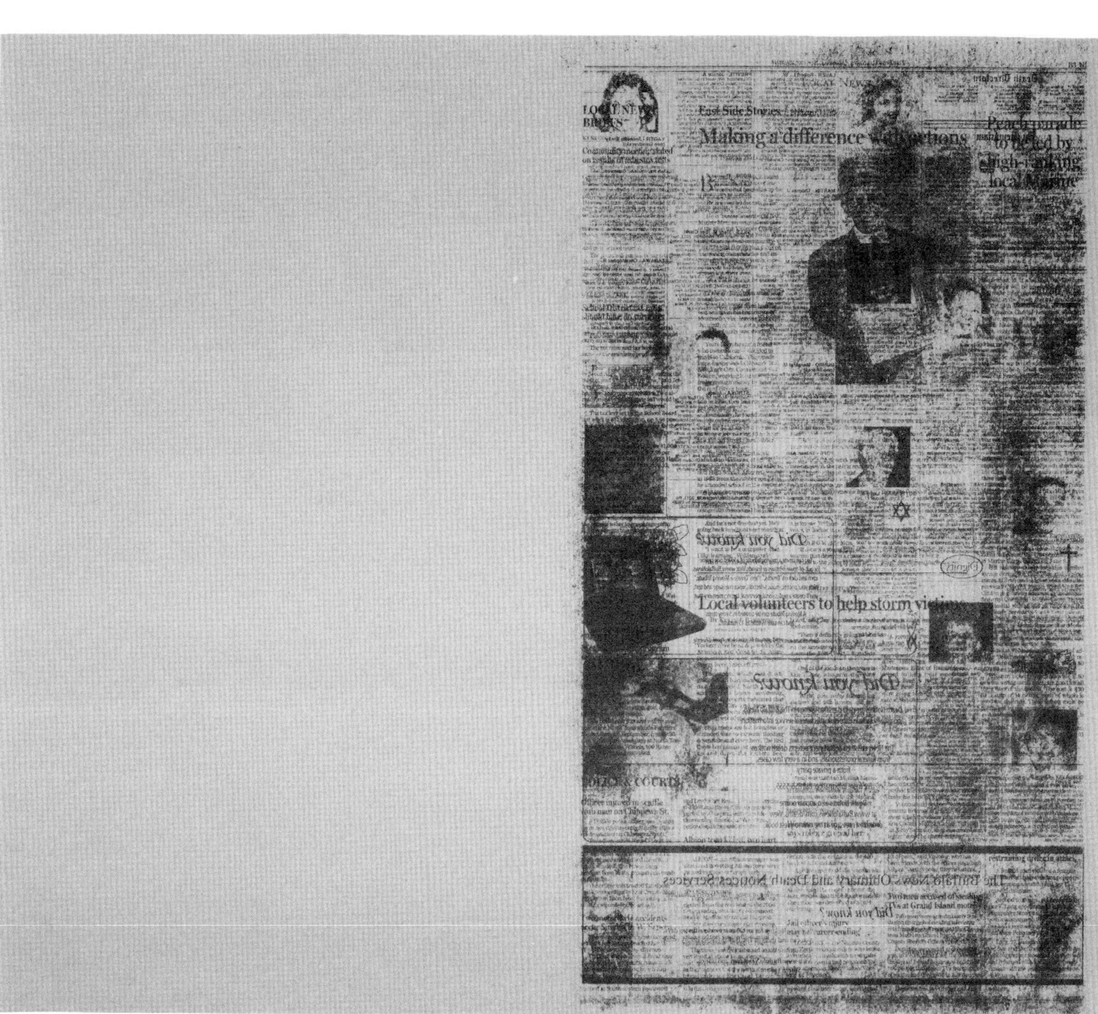
LOCAL NEWS BRIEFS
East Side Stories
Making a difference with actions
Peace parade
Local volunteers to help storm victims
Did you know?
Did You Know?
POLICE & COURTS
The Buffalo News: Obituary and Death Notices Services

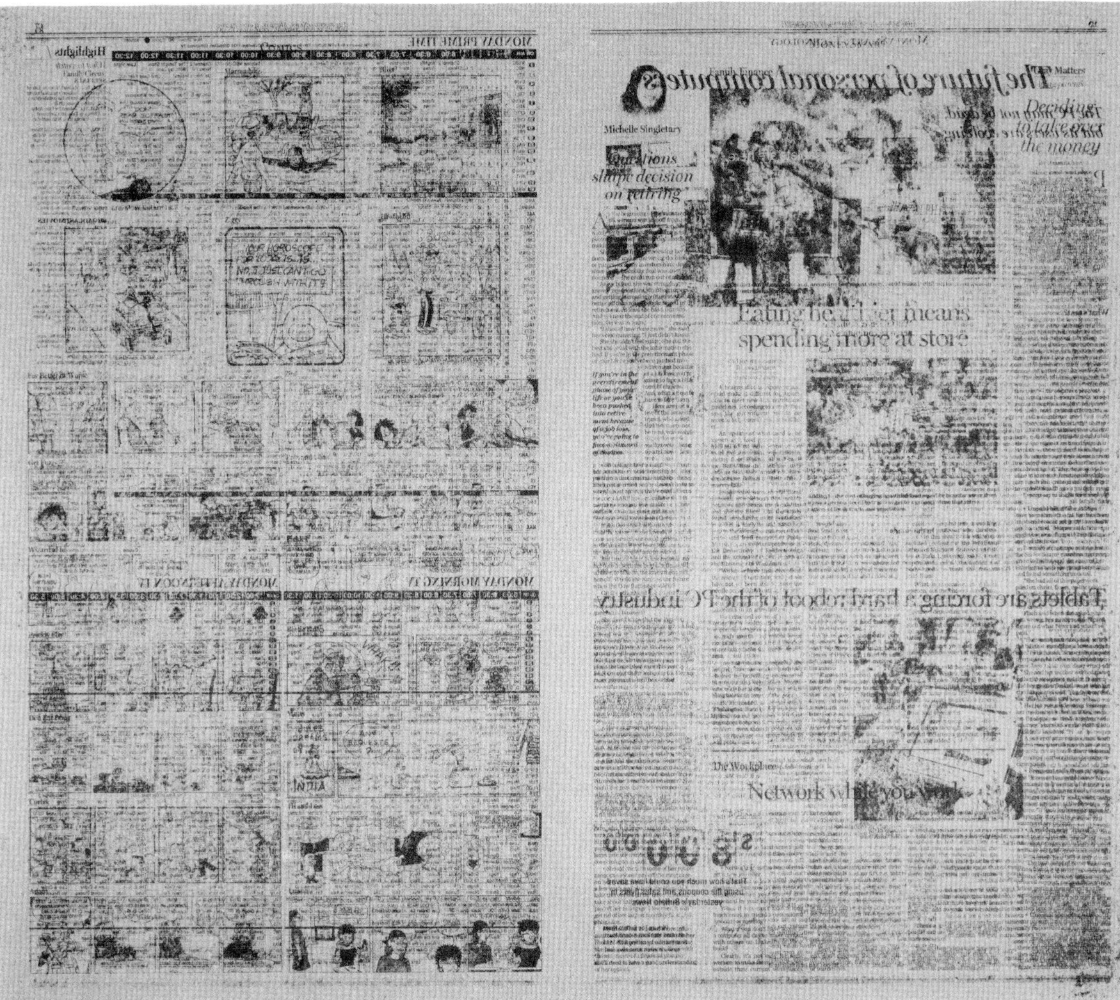
The future of personal computers
Michelle Singletary
Eating better diet means
spending more at store
Tablets are forming a hard reboot of the PC industry
Network while you work

Long ball helps Yankees earn split

Accident ruins Michael's run

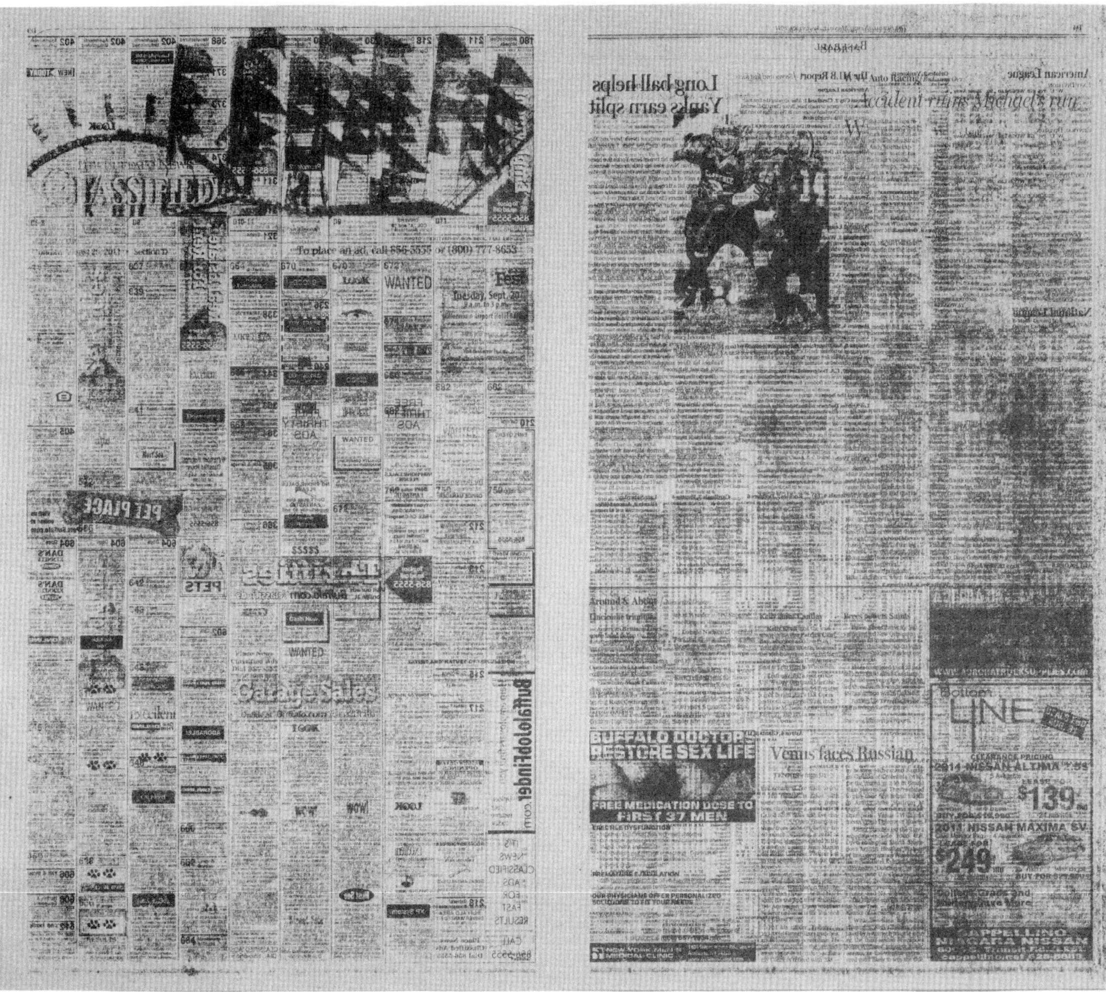

Venus faces Russian

BUFFALO DOCTOR RESTORE SEX LIFE

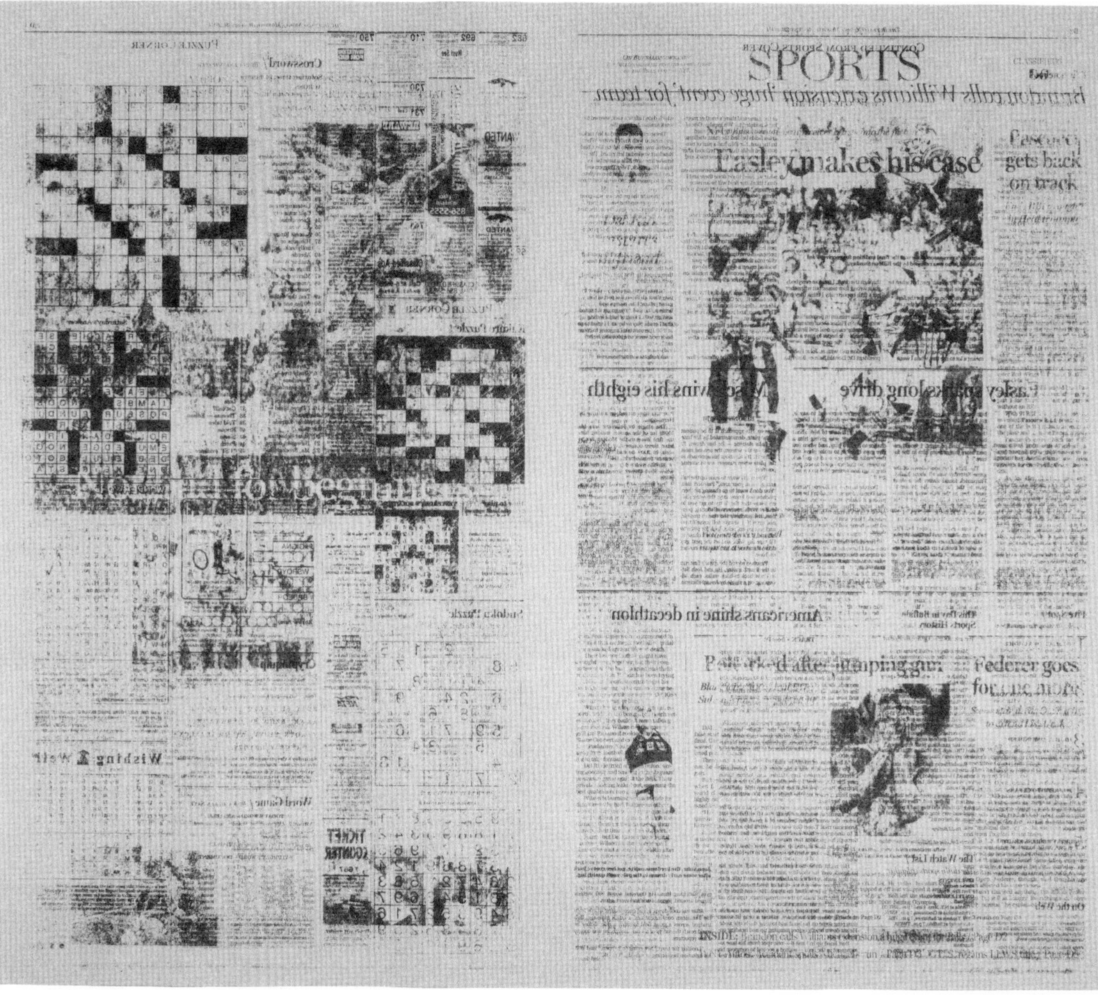

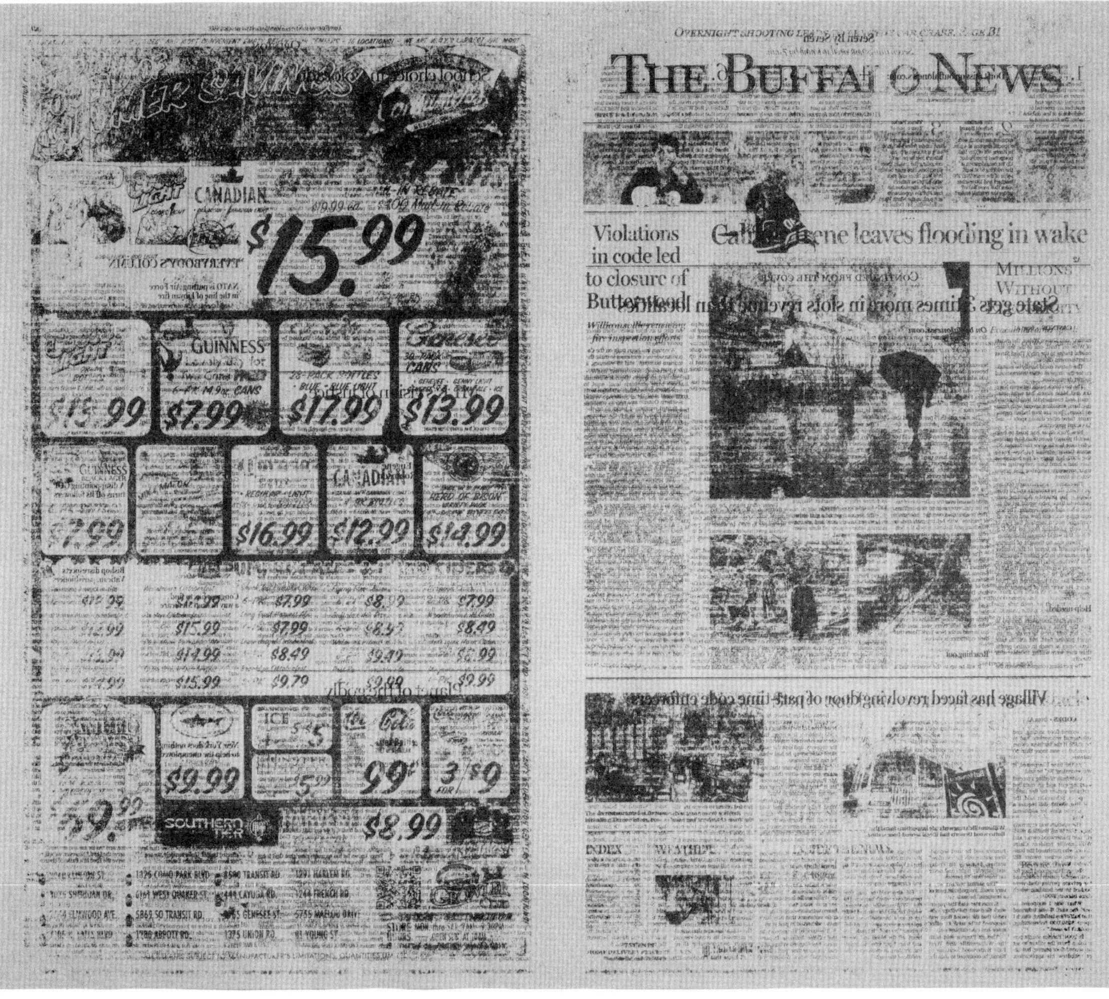
THE BUFFALO NEWS
Violations in code led to closure of Butterwood
Gale...ene leaves flooding in wake
State gets 3 times more in slots revenue than liberation
MILLIONS WITHOUT
Village has faced revolving door of part-time code enforcers
INDEX   WEATHER
CANADIAN
$15.99
GUINNESS
$7.99
$17.99
$13.99
$16.99
$12.99
$14.99
$9.99
$8.99
SOUTHERN TIER

47 states enact new laws on voting

Some pass, change...

Plan to ban plastic foam containers opposed

Arlington graves mix of discrepancies

World Trade Center site didn't lose a single

Indiana vouchers spur change in life of students

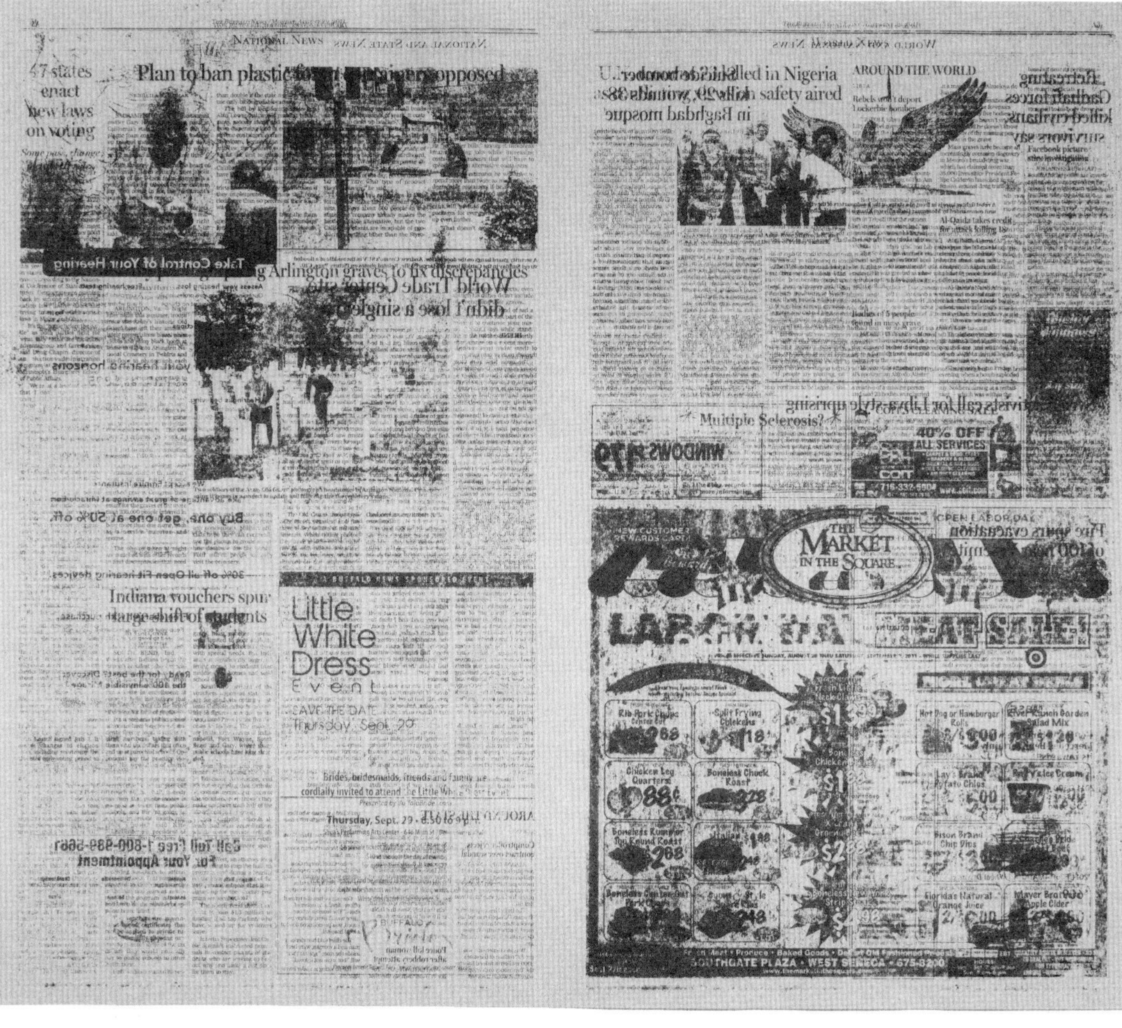

killed in Nigeria; safety aired in Baghdad mosque

AROUND THE WORLD

Rebels won't deport Lockerbie bomber

Al-Qaida takes credit for attack killing 18

Retreating Gadhafi forces killed civilians, survivors say

Facebook picture sites...

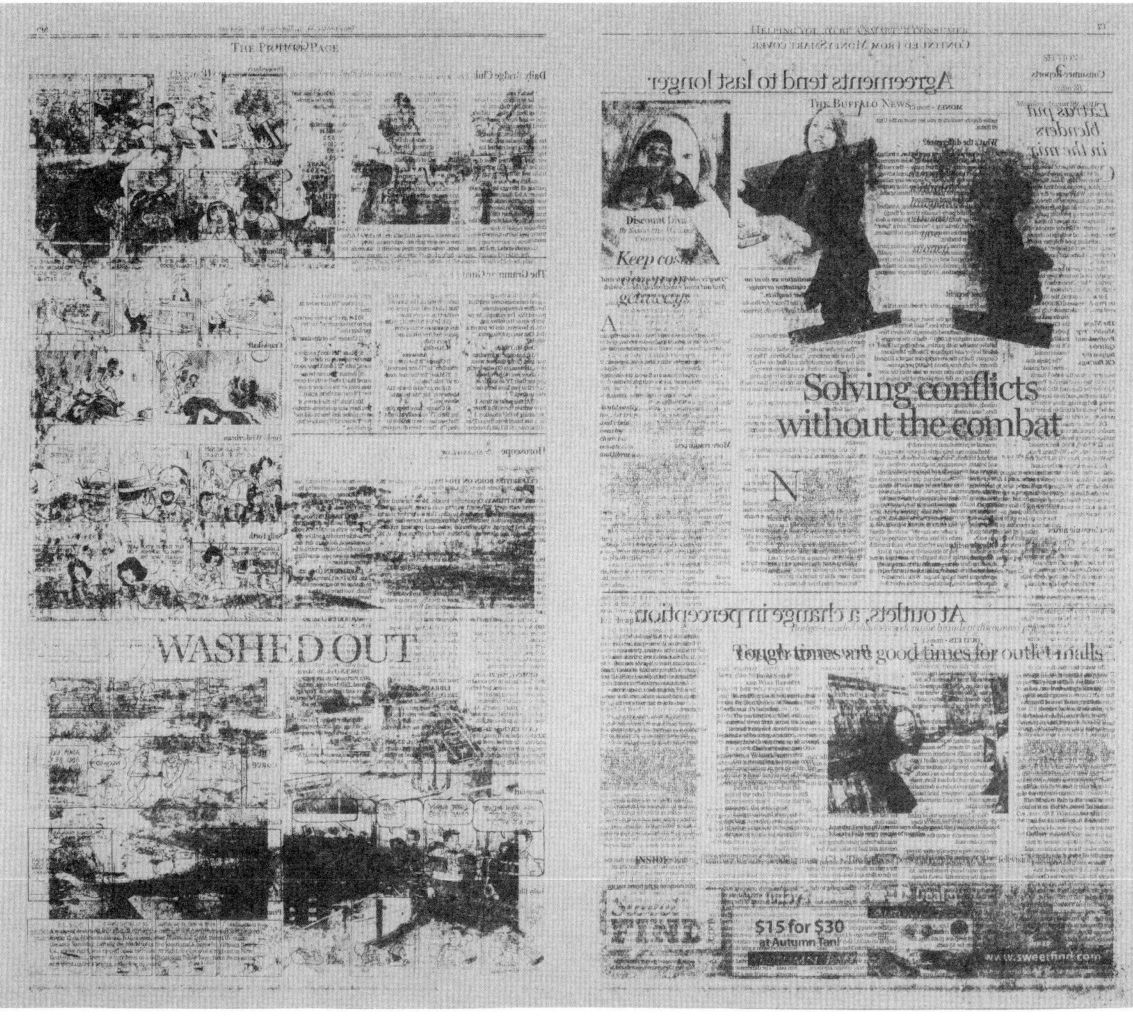
WASHED OUT
Agreements tend to last longer
Solving conflicts without the combat
The Buffalo News
At outlets, a change in perception
Tough times good times for outlet shops
$15 for $30 at Autumn Tan!
www.sweetfind.com

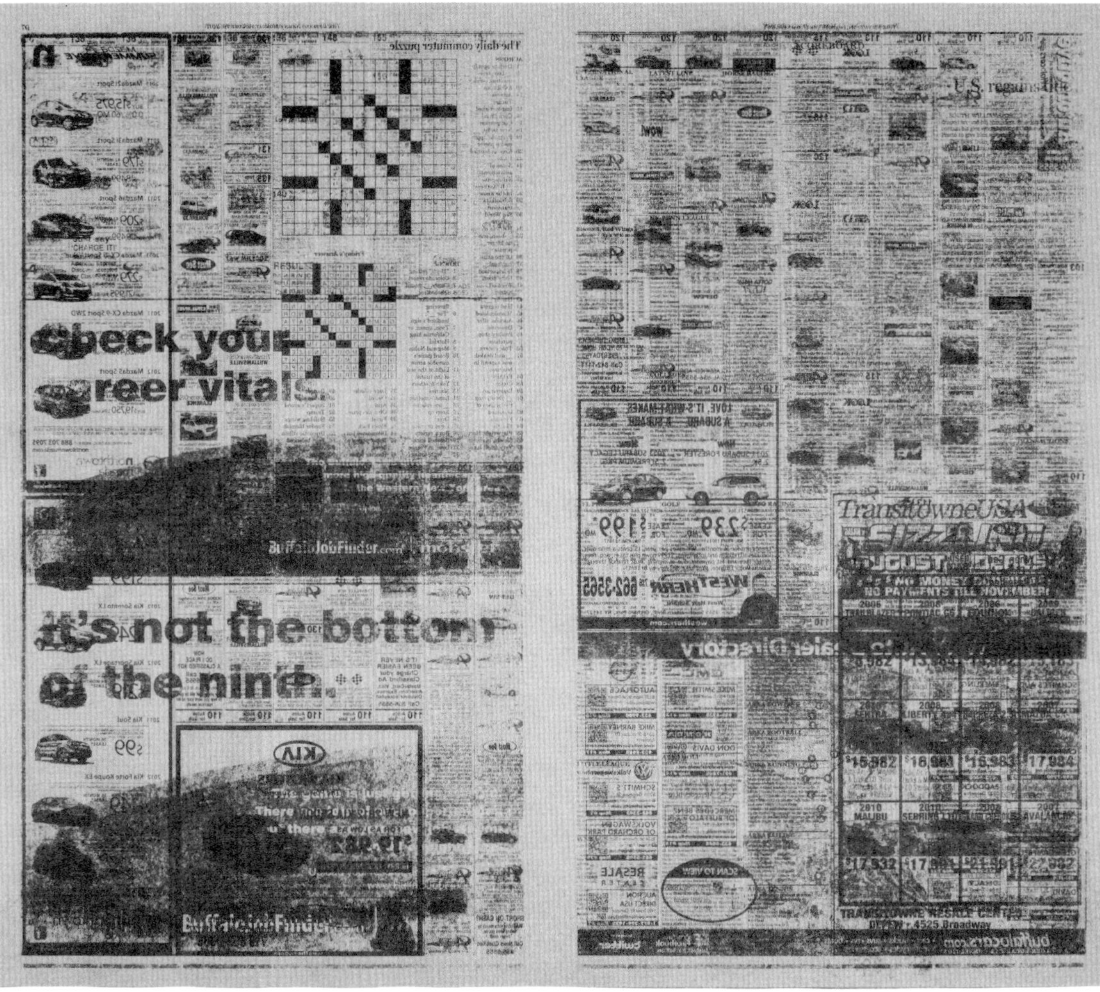

There are really only two kinds of jobs at Niagara: heavy industry and tourism. I got a job in tourism. Early in the spring of 1986, I was hired by Gray Line Tours, Incorporated, licensed by the state of New York and the province of Ontario. I had to pass a couple of simple tests. The Canadian, or Horseshoe, Falls are 158 feet high. The American Falls are 184 feet high and have a crest line of 1,060 feet. 30,000 cubic feet of water pass over both falls every minute during the daylight hours in the summer months. The water at the base of the falls is as deep as the falls are high.

I became Niagara Parks commission tour guide number 674. All that spring, summer, and fall, I drove van loads of tourists to all points of interest in the region. Every tour a three-hour tour, three times a day, 21 times a week. Did you go on the boat, I'm often asked. Yes, I went on the boat three times a day, 21 times a week.

Today, I know that in family photo albums in India and Japan there are pictures of me pointing out a geologic feature, telling a tale of daredevilry, posed with the rest of the tour group, the natural wonder in the background providing the perfect backdrop.

When I was a kid we visited the falls often, nearly every weekend, usually just before Sunday supper at Grandma and Grandpa's. Yet I never really got over my terror of the falls. Despite the fact that I led tours at Niagara Falls three times a day every day for a single summer, I never got over my terror of them. The water there is so swift, the drop so sudden. You can't stand there at the brink—watching the water roll over, changing yet always the same—you can't stand there without the thought crossing your mind. It would be so easy, so peaceful, to just jump. And it does happen. Often. Everyone who lives here has a story of someone they've seen, of someone they've heard about, of someone they've known who was killed in the falls.

Sometimes people will plan for a long time for a trip to the falls. They stand there watching the water for a while. Usually they'll remove their shoes, place their belongings, their personal effects, inside their shoes, climb up over the railing, and jump. I've seen it happen once. It was terrible—a young woman.

I was at Table Rock, guiding a tour. There was commotion as the would-be be rescuers ran past us. There were people on the observation deck calling out to the people on the Maid of the Mist boat trip who were taking photos of the majestic cataract, waving to the people 158 feet above, people who had seen her jump and were now trying to get the tourists aboard the boat to help the woman who was now being tossed about in the swirling waters. Her body was sucked behind the curtain of water. Disappeared. I don't know if they ever found her body. Sometimes they don't.

They pay people to go down to the lower river and retrieve the bodies they do find. $100 a body.

WES HILL

I think it started back in my grandfather's day. He did a lot of hunting and a lot of fishing. Them days they used to hunt below the falls. And being he was around the river all the time, any time they had someone jump over the falls, commit suicide, or someone drowned accidentally, or someone would fall over the cliff, they'd get my grandfather to go down and recover the bodies, or if the person was injured, to find them and get the help to bring them up. Well, then from there, it went to my dad.

Now when I was eight or nine years old, I used to go down with my dad when he pulled bodies out. I'd just stand back and watch. He did the same to all my brothers. And I got three boys and a daughter. And all my boys used to go down with me to retrieve the bodies, too, help us carry them up and everything.

ALIX SPIEGEL

Wes Hill collects the dead bodies of people who go over the falls. A warning: some of his descriptions may be a little graphic for some listeners.

break

After you see one or two or three, you get used to it. It's just like looking at a dead animal, really, because ninty percent of these people committed suicide. And it wasn't accidental. They wanted to be there, so why feel sorry for them? And it gets so after you've taken out a hundred or so, then it's just like somebody repairing a car. It's the same thing over and over again. And I've taken around 400 bodies out of the river.

One time, it was in the afternoon. I was going to collect my paycheck, and it was too early to get my paycheck. I had to wait a couple hours. My wife was with me, so I said, let's drive down to the Maid of the Mist, and I'll go look around the driftwood, see what's floating in there, because I got all kinds of fish and tackle and boat parts and everything out of the driftwood years ago. So as I parked car in the parking lot of the Maid of the Mist, I could see something pink going around the point just below the Maid of the Mist docks. There's a point of a rock that sticks out. I told my wife that looked like someone's back or something.

So I walked in behind one of the docks and I got a pike pole—it's a logger's pole they have to pull out driftwood—I got that, and I walked around the bay and went in behind this big rock. And here's an old woman laying there in the water. So I grabbed her by the arm and pulled her up onshore. Her body was still warm and everything, but her back was all smashed. She was dead. Apparently somebody in Montreal went to visit his mother and father, and he went in the house and there's a suicide note on the table saying that one didn't want to live without the other. And being they're up in their 70s, they figure one could die any time, so they said they're going over Niagara Falls and jump together. And they did. We got her body that day and I got the man's body about a week later.

I got an 18-year-old girl out of the river. She got pregnant and her boyfriend said he'd marry her. And then he didn't, and she accidentally caught him with another girl. And, she jumped over the falls. And of course, with the pressure on the body, when I went to pull her body out, the baby was halfway out. That is sickening.

Back in 1950, my brother Red decided he was going to try to go over the falls in a barrel. And he figured he needed something light, that if it hit any rocks, it would bounce so he wouldn't get hurt. So he got these big truck inner tubes, and he had them all put together with nylon webbing and everything, and a large net over the whole thing. The ends were closed with smaller inner tubes.

And he figured if he went over in this thing made with inner tubes— and he called it the Thing—that he'd come out all right. So I told him, I'm not going to help you. And he said, why? I said, mainly because you weigh more than the barrel you're going over in. And I said, those inner tubes, when you go over the falls, it's going to hit the water and stop dead. And I said, you're going to shoot right through it, right out of it. No, no, he says, I'll be all right.

I seen him that morning when he left my house. I was with my mother. And I went down to the Maid of the Mist landing with my brothers and my mother, because they figured he'd come out all right and they wanted to be there to greet him. And I was standing on the dock of the Maid of the Mist when I seen this jumble of tubes come out. And I turned to my mother and said, Bill's dead. She said, how do you know? I said, look at the tubes. They're all smashed up. And the small boat from the Maid of the Mist pulled the tubes in. He wasn't in it. They got his body the next morning.

My mother had been fighting my father and us boys for years. Every time we'd go down to the whirlpool, take a body out or rescue somebody, she'd say, you're going to get in trouble. Stay home. She'd worry about us all the time we were gone. She always did that. When my brother said he was going over the falls, two of the neighbors said, why don't you try to stop him? She says, ain't no sense in talking to my family. She says, see? I can't talk him out of it. She tried, but we're all bullheaded.

05.01—1998

ALIX SPIEGEL

Did she hate the falls or did she—

WES HILL

She hated it. She really hated it. My other brother Norman, he worked on the Maid of the Mist for years, and when they started the hydro project, he went to work in the hydro. And he was down working in the tunnels, and a rock came down one of the shafts and hit him on the head and killed him. So, actually, he was killed working along the river, too.

There's a legend for retelling by tour guides. I would retell this legend at the base of the Bridal Veil Falls during the Cave of the Winds trip part of my tour. This is a legend.

Every year the Indians who lived at the falls would, in the autumn, choose a maid to be sacrificed at Niagara to appease the angry god who lived in the waterfall, to ensure safe passage through long, cold, dark winter months. Now, it happened one year that the kind chief's only lovely daughter was selected as the maid of sacrifice. The chief loved his daughter very much. And though it broke his heart, he went through with the preparations. When the fateful day arrived, the canoe, beautifully painted and laden with garlands of flowers and cornucopias of nature's bounty, was carried to the village with his lovely only daughter inside. It was set into the river and she drifted away, silently, nobly, to her destiny.

When she hit the first rapids above the falls, she let out a small cry of terror, and her father, overcome by heartwrenching grief, jumped into his own canoe in hopes of rescuing her. As her canoe tossed and turned in the rapids, she called out again and again. The chief paddled faster, but alas, he was too late. With a final cry, she passed over the brink and was lost. Her father paddled with speed to the edge and he too, disappeared. It is said that the roar that you hear at the falls is the father crying out in anger, and the mist you feel raining down are her tears.

I would retell this legend three times a day every day to Australian and German tourists, to visitors from Tokyo and Bombay, to smiling blond-haired, straight-toothed families from Nebraska. They would smile and nod. Smile and nod. And then, simply because I could not help myself, I would tell them that the whole thing was a fabrication—not true at all.

The visitors, whether from Missouri or Melbourne, would lower their cameras, squinting at me, slack-jawed, like they were woken from a dream. I'd tell them that the aboriginal people who lived here never, ever engaged in human sacrifice of any kind, that really, what was in a way amazing about this story was that it survived for so long from the time of the very earliest tour guides in the area, from the 1820s, when Niagara was only just starting up.

What I didn't tell them was that I would, as a kid, attend the Maid of the Mist parade every summer. It came right down Main Street in Niagara Falls. And at the end of the parade every year, after the Shriners, the Knights of Columbus, high school bands, and waving dignitaries, the most elaborate float would appear—a re-creation of the Maid of the Mist legend, usually with a pretty young woman from the reservation nearby. There she'd be in her chicken wire and crêpe paper canoe, poised on the very brink of the paper mêché cataract, smiling, waving, throwing wooden nickels.

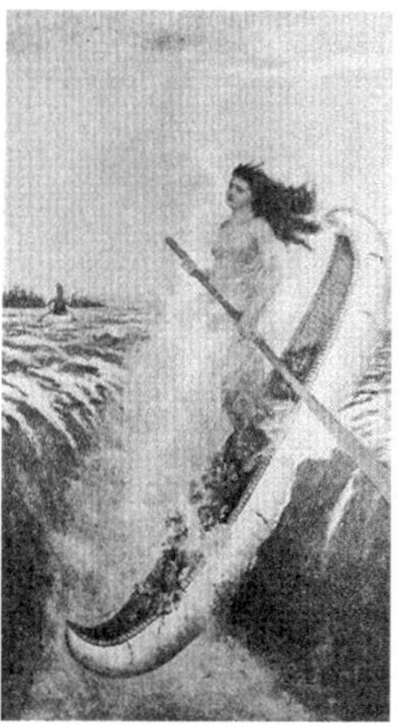

ALIX SPIEGEL

I met a man in a bar who told me a story about the city of Niagara Falls, which is the story I think of whenever I'm trying to explain Niagara to myself. He told me that the mayor of the city gets two things—a $30,000 salary and a license plate for his car. The license plate reads NF number one: "Niagara Falls number one."

A couple years ago, there was a mayor in Niagara who got voted out of office, but was so mad about being ousted that he refused to give the license plate to the new mayor. They argued back and forth and back and forth, the new mayor insisting the old mayor give the plate up, the old mayor refusing. Finally, said the man in the bar, the new mayor came up with a plan. He hired some men to steal the plate off the car of the old mayor. This, I should say, is unlikely. The new mayor was a policeman for 31 years, and he absolutely denied taking the plate. But the man in the bar said that he and many of his friends didn't believe the mayor. He said, this is the kind of town Niagara is. It's the kind of town where the new mayor steals the license plate off the old mayor's car.

•

Don Glynn is a newspaper man who's worked at the Niagara Gazette for 37 years, not including his time as a paperboy. He takes me on a tour of the city. We drive through downtown Niagara. There's not much driving to do. It's mostly a grid of empty lots. So we circle the same streets over and over, past the convention center, past the old Niagara Hotel, past the Wintergarden and the Rainbow Mall, past the convention center, past the old Niagara Hotel.

DON GLYNN

You see this big building here—the flashcube, we call it—that's the Occidental Chemical Center. There's very little occupancy in there anymore, because, well, Occidental has moved out for the most part. And the largest tenant in that nine-story building—this says something about the city of Niagara Falls—the largest tenant is the Small Business Disaster Assistance office.

All these places on both sides of the street for two or three blocks are just bars. And a lot of them are in Chapter 11. In fact, I often thought it would be neat to open a bar and just call it Chapter 11. It'd probably be packed with all the people that can't pay their bills.

ALIX SPIEGEL

Niagara was an industrial boomtown from the Twenties through the early Fifties, but in the late Fifties and Sixties, the electrochemical companies which lined the river found cheap power, nonunion labor, and lower taxes in other states. They left, and people left with them. Then, in the late Sixties and early Seventies, things got so bad that Niagara elected a flamboyant mayor with a plan.

The mayor was E. Dent Lackey and the plan was urban renewal. It was a simple plan which had three parts. Part one: the city would buy up

05.01—1998

all the property on the 82 acres of land which constituted Niagara's downtown area. Part two: the city would tear down all the property on the 82 acres of land which it had bought. And part three: developers from across America would flock to buy the empty lots, and they would build a new city. This plan is part of the reason it doesn't take very long to go on a driving tour of Niagara Falls. They only made it through parts one and two.

DON GLYNN

Everything was just kind of, like, leveled, and they thought that all these developers would come in and rebuild. And that didn't happen, because the developers weren't standing in line like this mayor thought they would be. They just didn't want to come here, and they didn't want to invest.

ALIX SPIGEL

So it was this one administration that just kind of leveled the city.

DON GLYNN

I thought he had a lot to do with it, Mayor E. Dent Lackey, for whom the plaza is named, by the way. You tear down a city and they name a plaza for you.

ALIX SPIEGEL

Don turns a corner and drives us past the Lackey Plaza, a large concrete square with a shallow white wall around it, in front of Niagara's convention center. He points to the corner of the wall where there's a smooth bronze plate.

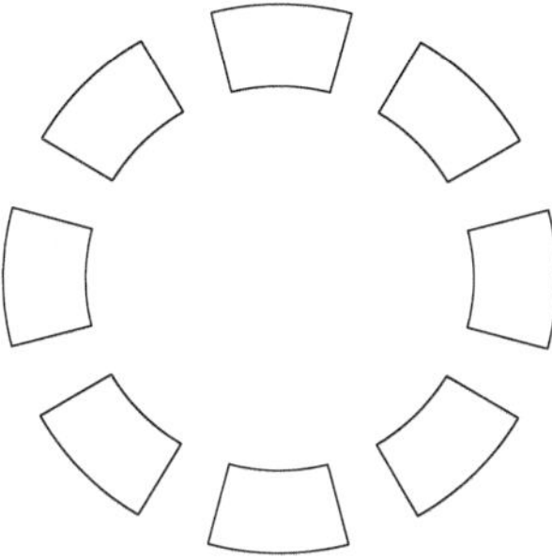

Sketch for *Untitled*, 2011

31

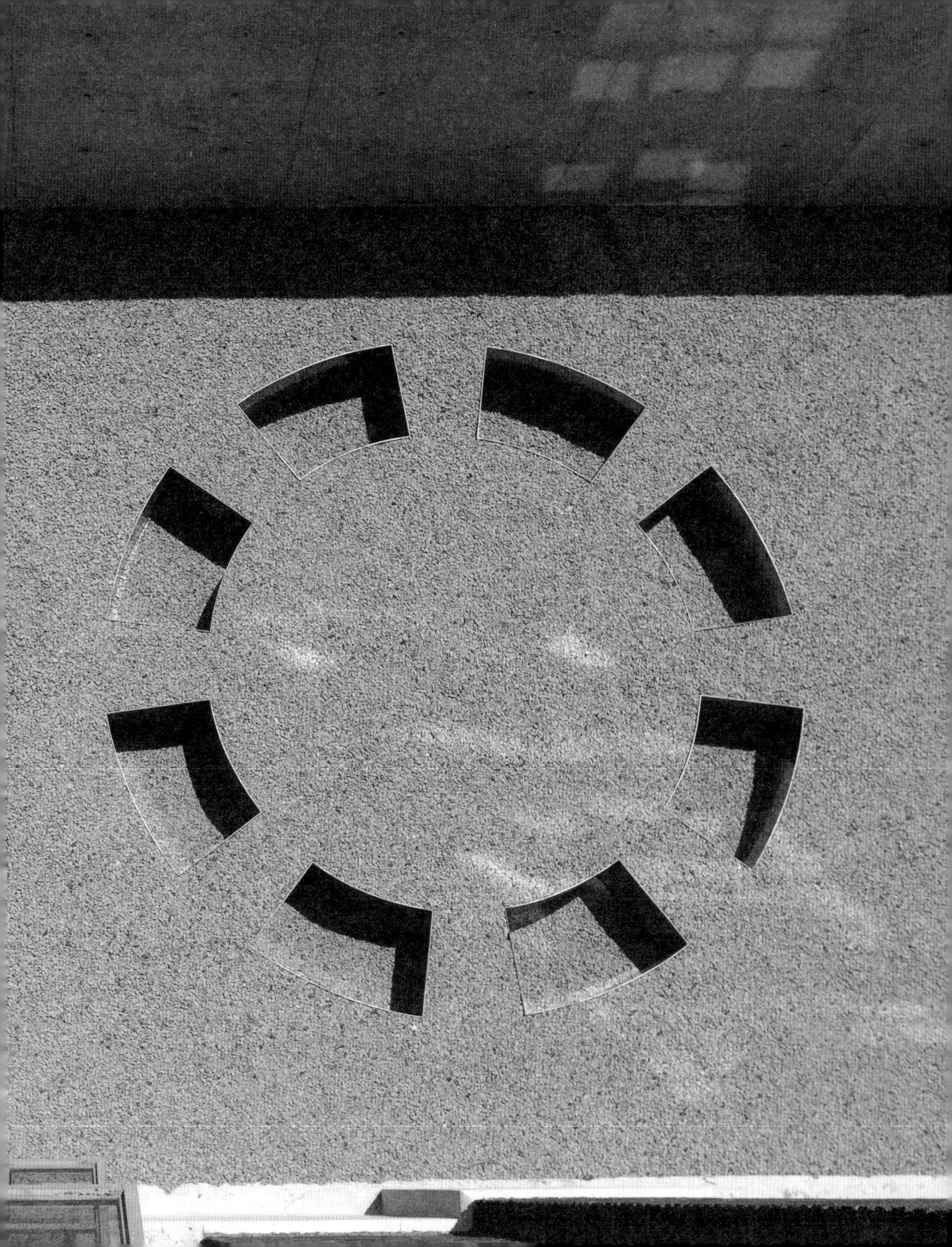

DON GLYNN

See that marker there, on the end there? See that little plate there? It looks like just an empty space.

ALIX SPIEGEL

Uh-huh.

DON GLYNN

Somebody stole the plaque. That's the Lackey Plaza, and that was the only proof that that was the Lackey Plaza, and someone stole it. It's been gone for, like, half a dozen years, the Lackey Plaza plaque. Does that tell you something about the city? Isn't that pathetic? I mean, somebody felt that strongly about it that they removed the plaque. But that tells you something.

ALIX SPIEGEL

We drive up the street a ways, past two enormous parking complexes a couple of blocks from the falls. They are pristine structures, four-story garages which take up two entire city blocks and dwarf everything around them.

DON GLYNN

We've got these ramp garages, and they've never really been filled. They've never been used, and they're free. You notice that? Yeah, because it was foolish to try to charge. Finally they put a fee on this one here, but that's only because they're trying to take advantage of the people that work in the office building across the street. But the one closest to the falls is free. You can walk in there, and all the levels are free. It doesn't cost anything. And yet all the booths are in place there and the electronic system and the cars. They spent a lot of money on just setting up the mechanisms, and they don't use it.

You got to remember that this is probably the capital of pipe dreams. I don't know why that is. You could go over to Navy Island, which is close by. It's around five miles away. That was one of the sites suggested once

05.01—1998

for the home of the United Nations. I mean, that's big thinking and big planning, right? Of course it never happened because the Rockefellers donated the land in New York. But they actually thought they could get the United Nations here.

More than half of Niagara's population has left since the Fifties. With industry gone, Don tells me about two-thirds of the population of Niagara Falls is on some form of public aid, and almost 60% of its population is elderly.

DON GLYNN

Young people do not stay here. They move out.

ALIX SPIEGEL

So in another let's say 20 years, you're going to have an entire city full of 80-year-olds. This is going to be like a huge retirement village or senior citizen's village.

DON GLYNN

Absolutely. No question. I think you're right. Young people just don't come in here and don't stay here.

ALIX SPIEGEL

And then, 25 years from now, it's going to be a ghost town, isn't it?

DON GLYNN

Well, it has all the makings of that, yeah.

break

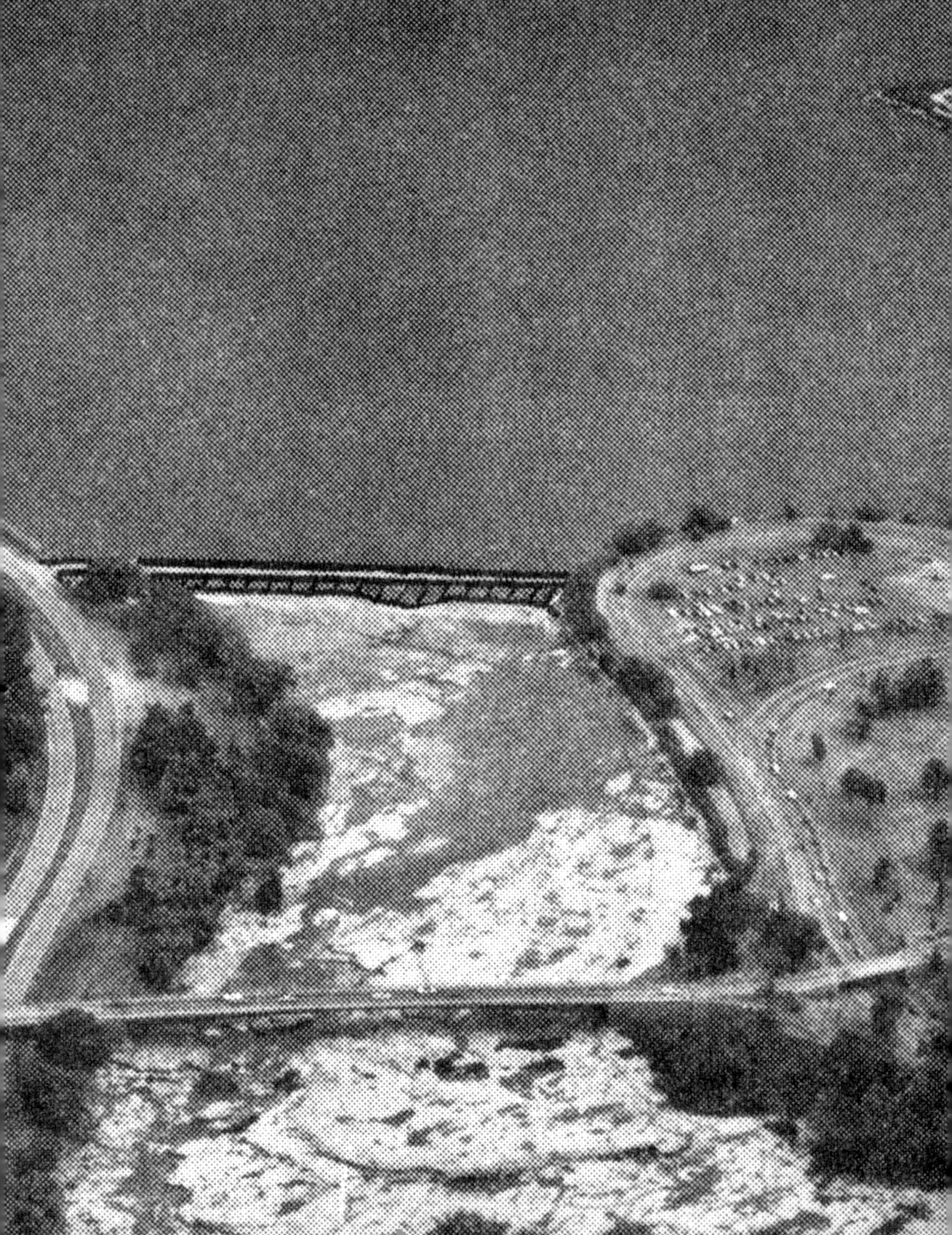

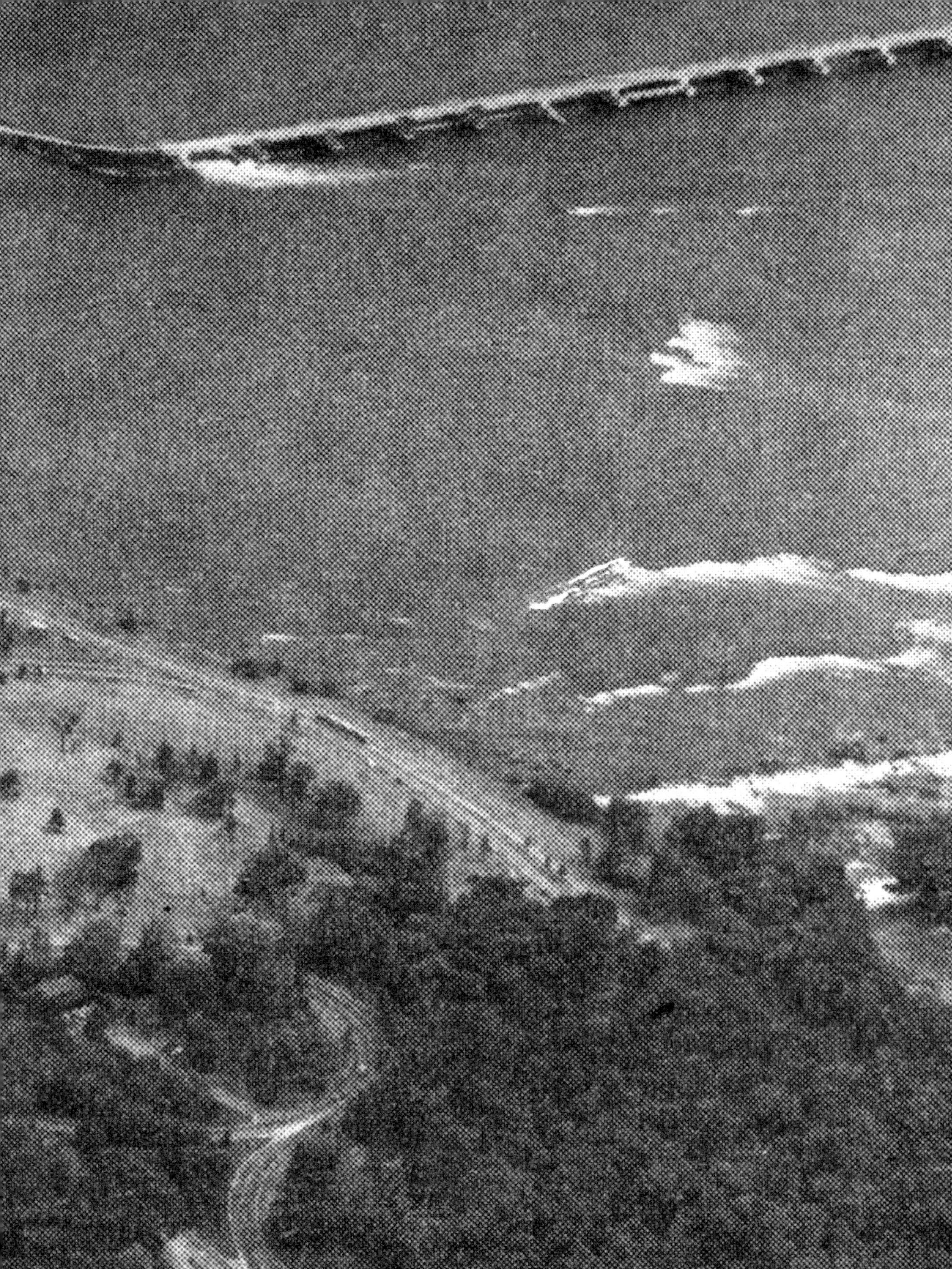

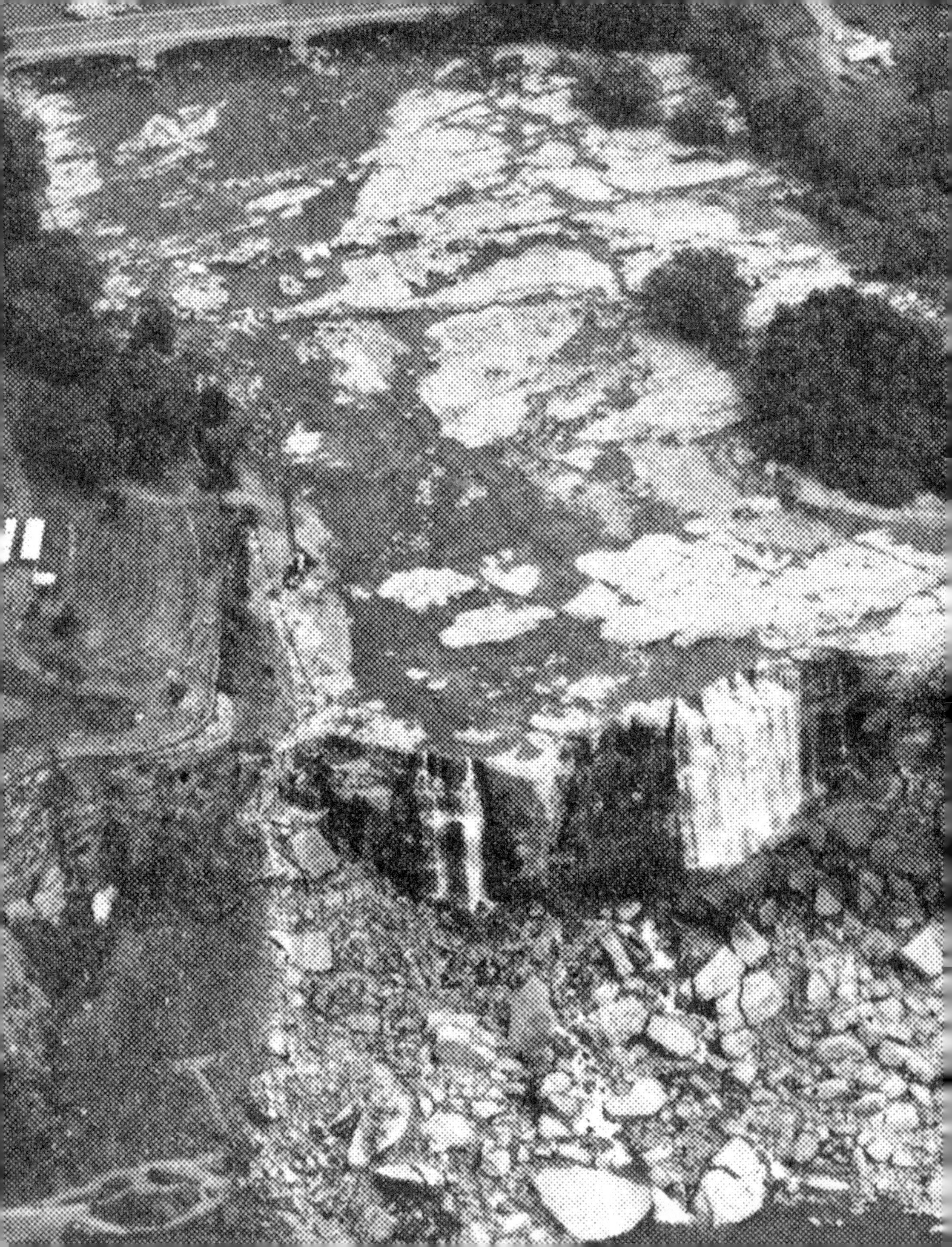

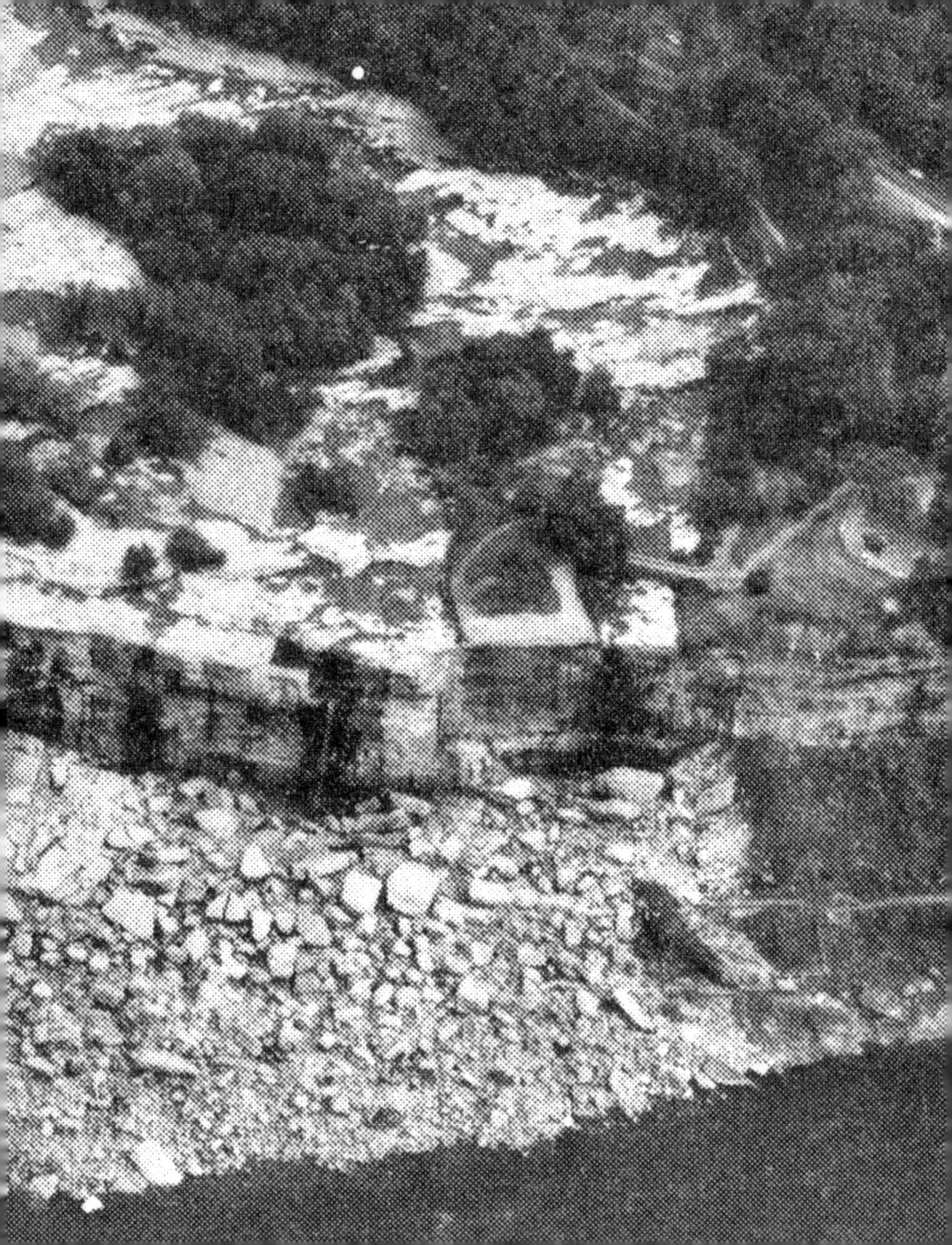

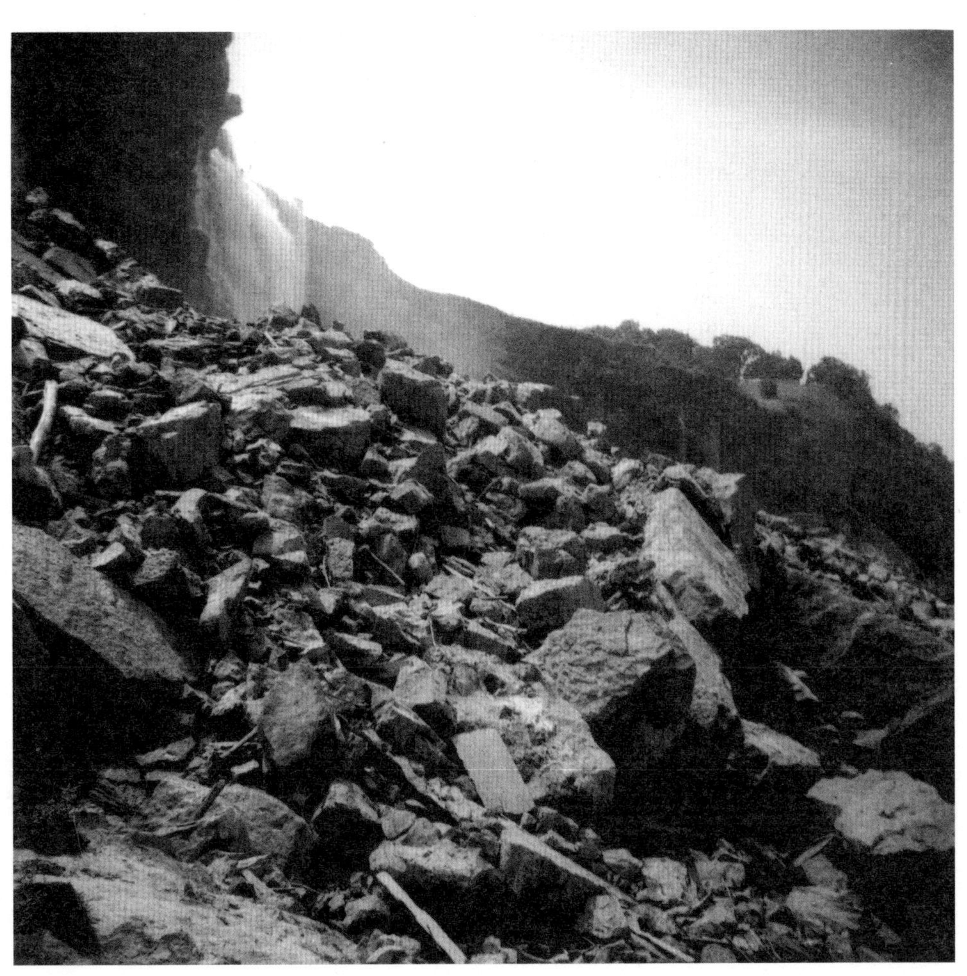

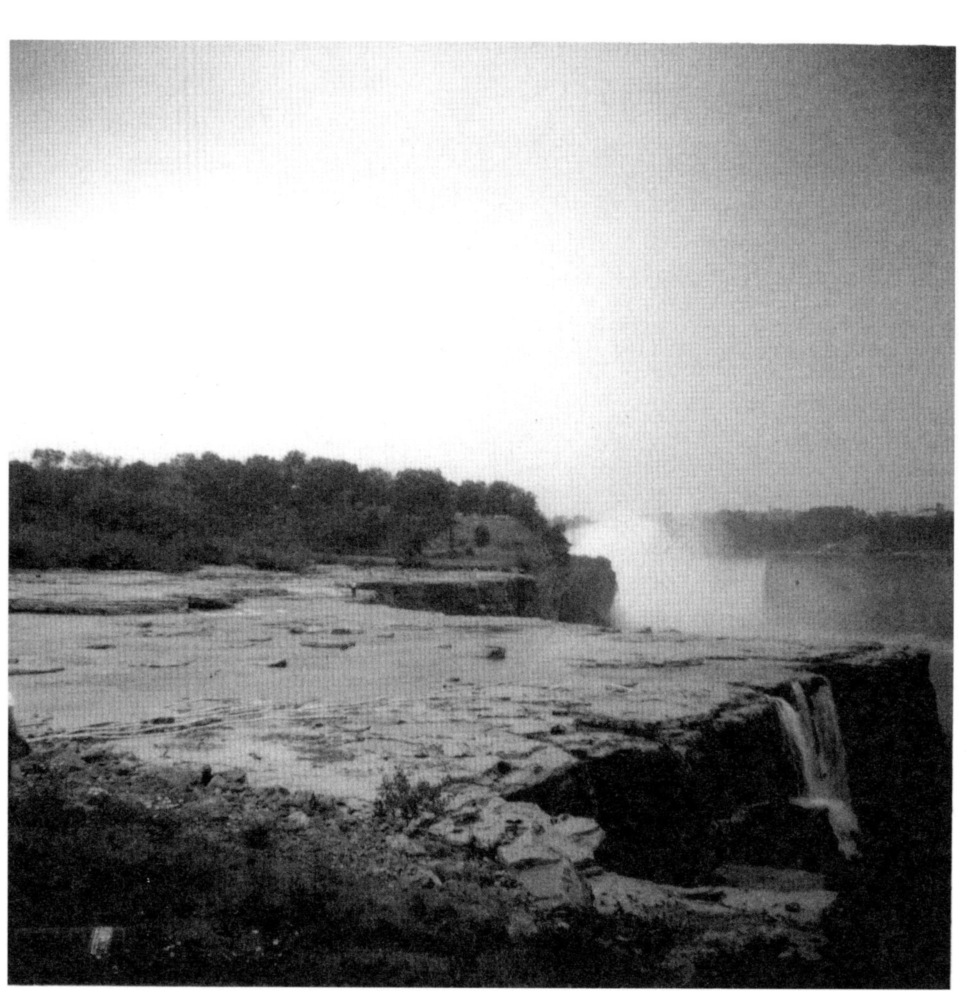

It's *This American Life.* I'm Ira Glass. Each week on our program: of course, we choose a theme, bring you a variety of stories on that theme. Today's program, Niagara. Stories from documentary producer Alix Spiegel, who visited the falls, and from David Kodeski, who grew up there. In one sense, the story of Niagara Falls is the story of how we as Americans relate to nature. We revere it and romanticize it on the one hand, and we try to exploit it on the other.

It's no accident that one of our country's most famous ecological disasters, Love Canal—where so many toxic chemicals were dumped that residents had to be evacuated—is just a few minutes' drive from the falls. Those chemicals were there because so many factories grew up near the falls, near the cheap hydroelectric power provided by the falls. And that's where our story continues.

break

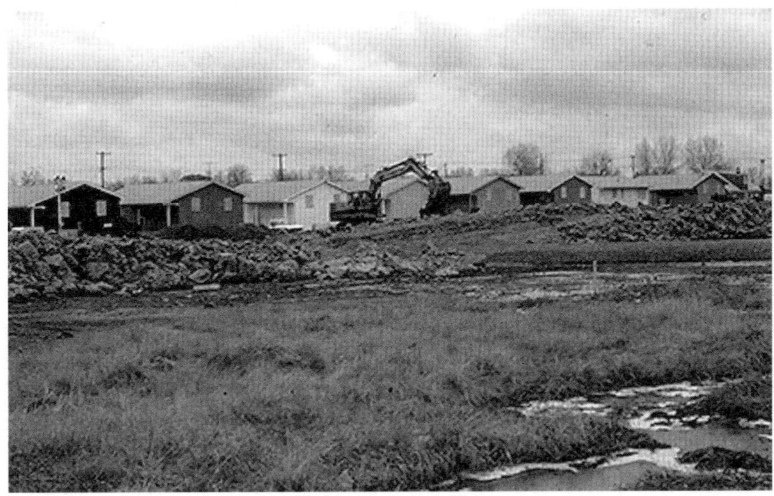

Cheap, plentiful hydroelectric power lured the electrochemical industries of the world to Niagara. My father worked 40 years or so for DuPont in the sodium facility there. My uncle Ray worked for Carborundum, my cousin Paul for Union Carbide, my cousin Carl for Goodyear Tire and Rubber, my uncle Matt for Occidental Chemical and Petroleum, formerly known as Hooker Chemical.

The factories line the Niagara River not far from the falls themselves. When I was driving tours that summer, we were instructed to direct the attention of our guests toward the river to point out the wideness of the river, to point out the relative calmness of the water. We were instructed to keep the attention toward the river and away from the chemical factories belching yellow and white smoke. None of this would appear in the official tour guide training manuals, of course, but the veteran guides who trained us reminded us that we were working for tips. And who would tip a tour guide who pointed out a ravaged and polluted landscape?

Someone whose attention had drifted to the east might ask, what are those factories? And we were then instructed to explain how during the war effort these plants had supplied the armed services to aid in beating the Axis powers, and those nylons GIs were plying Euro cuties with were made right here in Niagara Falls.

The summer I turned 17, there was a great deal of family talk about which plant I should work for, just for the summer, see if I like it. The money's good. The money is very good. But I did not want to work in any one of the factories under any circumstances. They seemed deadly. I knew that my grandfather retired early because of his failing health. He died of pancreatic cancer in 1966.

My grandfather was a chemical operator. He ran what they called caustic—caustic and chlorine. They make drain cleaner out of it, detergents—soap too. They use it to purify water. My relatives say dioxin was in the air there. They say that when they made caustic, the vapor would go up and it would turn into caustic dust. They say it was everywhere, even in the place where they ate. They say you could write your name in the dust on the table. You'd leave your coffee cup on the table and there'd be a mark.

05.01—1998

I spent a lot of time sitting on the front porch of my parents' house staring, at the factories on the horizon—towers, ironworks, smokestacks. You could also see the mist of the falls from there, but you couldn't be sure if it was the mist you were seeing or the smoke from the factories. Near my parents' house, kids would play on the sites of abandoned factories and dump sites. They called them the whites because everything there was thick with white ash. It's hard to say what this did to people. If you look at the studies, Niagara's cancer rate is higher than other areas, but just a little.

He went in and out of the hospital for months. One night when Tom was home from the hospital, we were all watching a movie on television, Karen Black in *Trilogy of Terror*, the one where she gets chased around her apartment by that little Zuni fetish doll. And Tom had to go to the bathroom. And we helped him down the hall and into the bathroom, and he had a seizure. He went limp. He passed out on the bathroom floor and his eyes rolled back into his head. We all started to cry.

break

That summer, Tom was given radiation therapy, cobalt treatments. We had to watch him. We had to take care of him. Sharon was taking care of him one afternoon, and they were playing with some toy soldiers in the yard. Sharon believes that Tom knew that he was dying. He was killing the already fallen soldiers, shooting them over and over. And Sharon said, why are you killing them like that? Well, he said, well, they won't suffer like that.

break

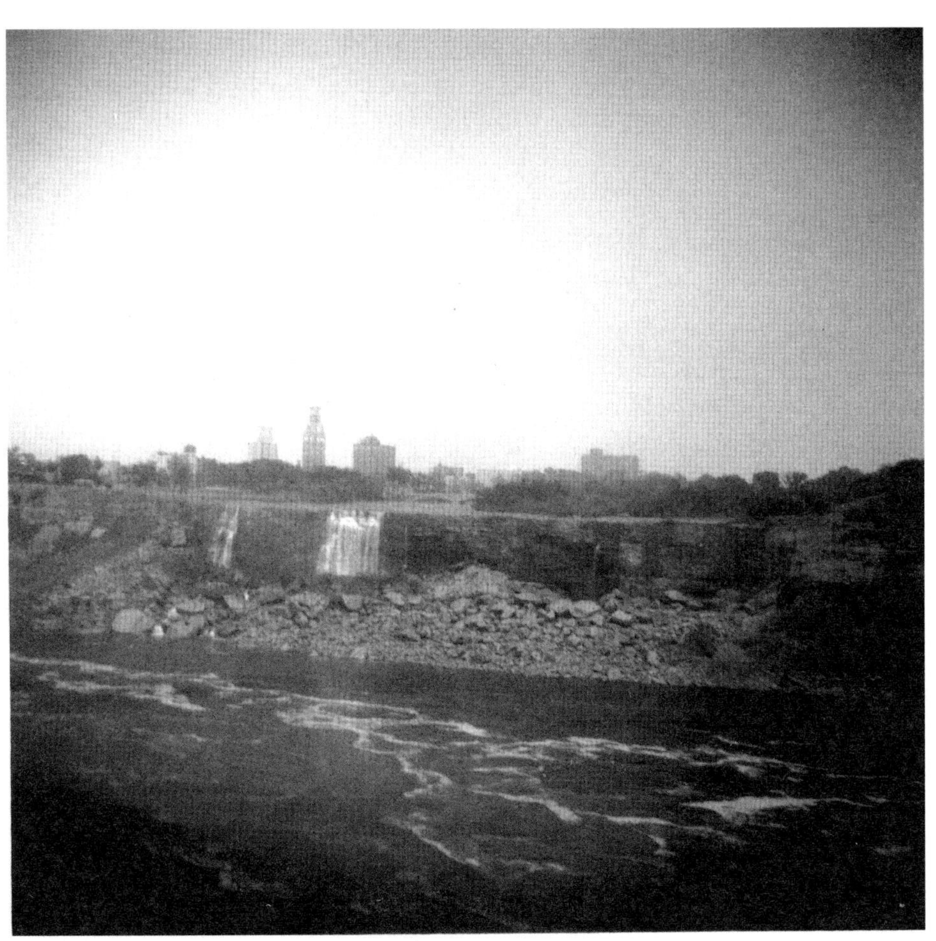

break

Death and love—that's what Niagara represents—the nexus of death and love. Suicides on the one hand, honeymoons on the other. When I told a friend I was going to Niagara Falls, he asked me if I was getting married. Four different people asked me that question. I told them all I had no immediate plans. Then I called 1-800-785-LOVE, the Niagara wedding chapel at the Radisson Hotel in Niagara Falls, New York.

The Niagara wedding chapel offers what they call a full-service wedding, which means that in addition to a ceremony with flowers, preacher, complimentary bottle of champagne, license, and wedding video, I'm entitled to a day of beauty at the hair salon next door and a discount on a room for my wedding night at the Radisson. Niagara, I was told, is the honeymoon capital of the world. The Niagara wedding chapel performs over 2,000 weddings annually.

At the end of our conversation, the man on the phone, who identified himself as the owner's brother, suggested that he and I get married. He told me he was single and I had a nice voice. I actually have his proposal in my notes of our conversation. There it is: right under the information about the twenty-four-hour waiting period, I wrote with a blue ballpoint pen, "Will marry me."

•

It's Catherine and A.J.'s first time, which is a little unusual for the Niagara wedding chapel. Most of their market is second marriages. Catherine and A.J. have driven to Niagara from Pittsburgh with 30 of their friends and family, and are now waiting together with their maid of honor in the welcome area outside the chapel. They all look happy and nervous. They're laughing and joking, talking about the kinds of things you talk about right before you get married.

WOMAN 1

A.J., you still have time to back out.

WOMAN 2

No.

CATHERINE

He's calmer than me.

WOMAN 1

I know. He's so calm. That's cool.

CATHERINE

I should have gone to the bathroom.

ALIX SPIEGEL

Chris, the owner and manager of the Niagara chapel, comes in to tell Catherine and A.J. that even though two of their guests haven't arrived, the wedding must start. He's got a 4:30. He can't wait anymore. Everyone hurries to their places while Chris makes a brief announcement to their guests. They're allowed to take pictures, but everyone must remain in their seats until the end of the ceremony. I barely have time to wonder why this last instruction is necessary before—

Music—"BRIDAL CHORUS" by RICHARD WAGNER

Catherine starts crying as soon as she enters the chapel. She cries her way to the altar, cries as she takes her [place] beside A.J., cries as the justice reads through the opening of the ceremony, cries more when the justice asks her if she'll love her husband through sickness and through health. The bareness of her emotion infects everyone in the room.

I see three people in the front row hunch their shoulders and bring their hands to their faces, then the man in the second row next to the wall, then the woman sitting next to him. It jumps the 12-year-old boy sitting next to her and moves to the third row, then the fourth. Now I am crying. We are all in the room crying. Everyone happy and flushed and sure that everything, everywhere, is going to be OK after all.

And then, six minutes and 47 seconds after it begins, it's finished. A.J. and Catherine are now husband and wife.

48

05.01—1998

MAN 1

Ladies and gentlemen, it is my great pleasure to introduce to you Mr. and Mrs. [UNINTELLIGIBLE].

[CHEERS]

ALIX SPIEGEL

In another 10 minutes they're gone. All evidence of the couple is removed, and the only sound in the chapel is the hum of fluorescent lights. Chris pops in a new video for the next couple and resets the video machine. He sets out a new bouquet and checks to see if the bride's dressing room is clean. Then his 4:30 arrives, Rod and Lori, just the two of them. No friends. No family. Lori goes to the bride's dressing room to check her makeup, and I try to talk to Rod. This is not an easy thing to do.

ALIX SPIEGEL

Where are you coming from?

ROD

New Jersey.

ALIX SPIEGEL

Oh, all the way up from New Jersey?

ROD

Right.

ALIX SPIEGEL

What brought you up here?

ROD

Well, Lori.

ALIX SPIEGEL

She wanted to come to the falls?

49

ROD

Right.

ALIX SPIEGEL

Had you heard about it?

ROD

Yeah, I think. You know.

MAN 2

He's very quiet.

MAN 3

He is.

ALIX SPIEGEL

Lori comes out, and she and Rod are introduced to the minister. There are handshakes and some uncomfortable laughter. Then—

Music—"BRIDAL CHORUS" BY RICHARD WAGNER

No one cries at this wedding. The two of them walk alone to the altar. The chapel is empty, just rows and rows of chairs. Rod and Lori stand stiffly as the preacher reads on and on. Rod seems perpetually awkward, not visibly happy at all. Lori isn't visibly happy either. As I've said, there's no one in the room, just a bunch of chairs and some video cameras. And it's hard not to wonder why they've chosen to engage in this exercise at all. It just seems so sad.

I look around the little stage that serves as a wedding altar, where all day long it's a series of these dramas in 30-minute intervals, one couple after another, some happy, some not. Then eight minutes after it began, it's over. Rod and Lori are husband and wife. No one's there to applaud.

50

Niagara, home of the two-tank honeymoon—one tank up, one tank back. That's what Chris tells me. He hands me a card which says, "Niagara, honeymoon capital of the world." But Niagara isn't the honeymoon capital of the world. It hasn't been for a long, long time. It held this title between the 1840s and the 1940s, when the railroads made Niagara a cheap and easy weekend getaway for newlyweds in New York, Pennsylvania, Ohio, New Jersey, all up and down the east coast.

But the railroad was discontinued decades ago, and affordable air travel makes destinations like Hawaii much more popular with newlyweds today. But the idea of Niagara as honeymoon capital remains in a hundred old movies and songs. And those movies and songs are a powerful force.

Chris tells me he gets calls from Florence, Italy; London, England; from Japan. In the office in the back of the chapel, there's an entire wall of pictures of happy couples who have been married by Chris. I look at the pictures. Chris gets ready for his 5 o'clock.

break

Here's another story we would tell as tour guides. This one happens to be true.

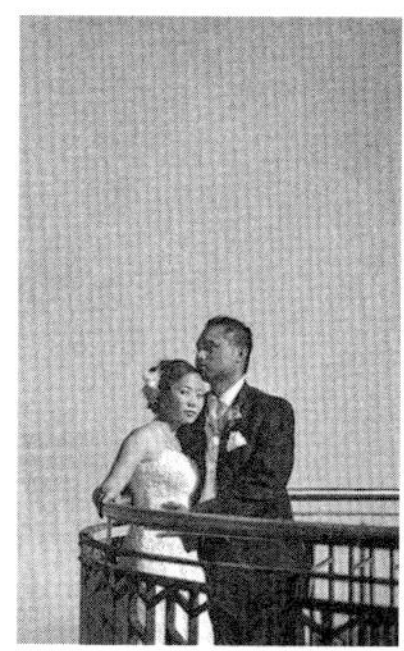

ANNIE EDSON

05.01—1998

Taylor was a 73-year-old school teacher from Bay City, Michigan. She arrived in Niagara sometime in the summer of 1903. She was alone, some say an old maid. She was penniless. She was desperate. She'd made up her mind that she would be the first person to go over Niagara Falls in a barrel and live. She designed and had built a special barrel. She hired a manager, one Frank M. "Tussy" Russell. Russell announced to the world that the 73-year-old Taylor was a widow, 42. Taylor met the press saying, I might as well be dead as remain in my present condition. It will be fame and fortune or instant death.

At half past 1 o'clock on October 24, 1903, Annie Edson Taylor squeezed into her barrel. Cold water inside the barrel sloshed around her ankles. Annie could feel the pull of the river, the swiftness of the rapids. Her barrel banged and scraped against the rocks above the falls. Annie, deafened by the roar of the river, prayed aloud. The barrel neared the crest of the mighty Horseshoe and hung there at the lip, seemingly stuck, hanging over the boiling chasm. The crowd gasped, held its breath, and then she dropped into the cataclysm, into the chasm, into the roiling tempest below. She was pulled out of the barrel below the falls, dazed, bleeding, but very much alive. A cheer went up from the assembled crowd. The woman is alive!

While Annie recuperated in a Canadian hotel, Frank M. "Tussy" Russell disappeared with Annie's barrel. He made his fortune with it and a beautiful young woman posing as Annie, queen of the falls.

Annie had another barrel built, posed for photos with it, told and retold her story to tourists for pennies. She wrote her autobiography. She aged on the streets of Niagara, told tourists she was a widow, 52. She became scary, died alone, a lady of good breeding and refinement.

This is a story of my hometown. The prevailing symbol of the town used to be the beautiful Indian Maid of the Mist, when really it ought to have been bad luck, down at the heels Annie Edson Taylor, a lady of good breeding and refinement who never got an even break.

break

PETER DEBERNARDI

You have to become one. I remember when the guys were working on my barrel, I used to stand back, stand aside and just psych into it. I used to do a lot of work on it myself. And that's the only thing keeping you from death. You become one. You actually acquire quite a relationship with a barrel, a piece of metal, that one will not understand unless they're there. That is saving their life. So you can imagine the psyching in and the unity that you have with this vessel.

ALIX SPIEGEL

Peter DeBernardi lives half a mile from the falls, so close that his windows sometimes rattle from the roar. One night in 1987, Peter was lying in bed listening to the falls, and it hit him. He would make history by going over the falls in a barrel built for two men, the first time ever two people would go over together.

He found a partner, a guy named Jeff, and together with a crew of men they built a three-thousand-pound deluxe steel barrel with inner tubes inside to cushion their fall, two windows of bulletproof glass so they could see out as they went over, and a stereo system so they could listen to tunes. They also installed a recording system so they could document the whole experience on tape. It took them 19 months to build. And then, as Peter will tell you, there was the mental preparation.

PETER DEBERNARDI

As far as psyching in, I used to sit out here on the front porch sometimes up to 3 o'clock in the morning, 4 o'clock in the morning, because it's just me and the falls. It's rumbling. Like I said, I'm only a half mile away. And it was so quiet. Now sometimes if the wind is right, the breeze is right, it carries the mist all the way down the gorge. You can see it's like a white wall that goes down the gorge. OK? I'm sitting there. And all of a sudden, there was this little finger of mist that left the mainstream of the mist, came over, and it hovered over the small [UNINTELLIGIBLE] across the street here. And it looked like two little fingers. And it was pointing—believe it or not—pointing right at me sitting there.

54

It stayed there for about 10 minutes. Then it finally, like a finger, as if you're just bending your finger back to the palm of your hand, it joined the rest of the mist. And that was it. Talk about getting in deep with this. It was trying to send me messages. And oh, god, what I went through mentally on this.

•

The night before, I came home. I was out doing a normal job during the day, and then I came home, had something to eat, went to bed, fell asleep, and woke up the next morning. I didn't wake up, nothing like that. I guess I was so mentally prepared, psychologically prepared, that it didn't bother me. As a matter of fact, around my bed, I used to have pictures of Niagara Falls. I used to stare into them to fall asleep. I never had any bad nightmares or nothing like that.

But next morning I got up, and Jeff was down. So we got everything together, the whole crew together. And the vessel was up at the crew chief's house. It was a great big state truck. And the barrel was on a special crib system on the truck. And I remember we climbed into it. And I will never forget the sound. And to this day, that sound remains in my mind. Them pounding those metal dog lathes. It was like being sealed into a metal coffin. And that was like, yeah, this could be it. This is your coffin.

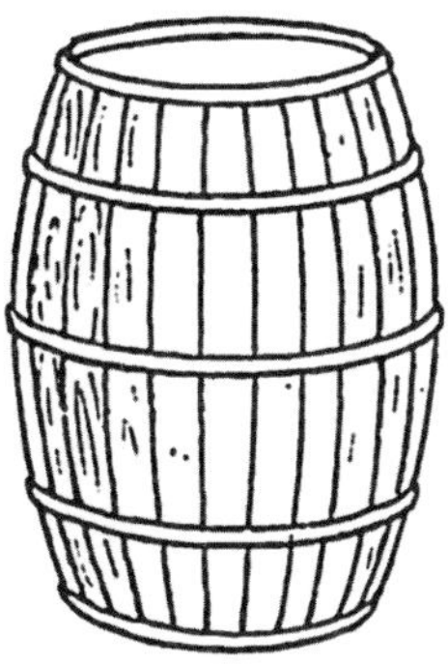

JEFF PETKOVICH

That's good.

PETER DEBERNARDI

So here we are. We're going down the road. That was the shortest two-mile trip ever in my life. We could hear each gear shift, each stop, each turn. I knew exactly where we were turning. And they went down Murray Hill and along River Road.

JEFF PETKOVICH

Feels like we're going down Murray Hill. Uh-oh.

PETER DEBERNARDI

OK. She's straight now, man.

JEFF PETKOVICH

OK, good. Guess what?

PETER DEBERNARDI

What?

JEFF PETKOVICH

We're [BLEEP] on River Road, I think, now.

PETER DEBERNARDI

No kidding.

MAN 4

55.

JEFF PETKOVICH

Yeah, there we go.

05.01—1998

And the truck pulled in, backed up. And they released the barrel, and they pushed it. And that's when it crashed into the water.

JEFF PETKOVICH

Uh-oh, Peter, we're there. We're there.

PETER DEBERNARDI

When you hit that water, this barrel weighing that much—a ton and a half, when we hit that river bed—it was about five feet of water. It slammed into the floor of it so hard that it, like, jolted the mind. It was benumbing to the mind. And I thought, oh, my god, we didn't even go over yet. We just hit the river.

Then I'm looking out of the glass. And here's a bunch of seagulls floating over. And I'm looking out through the bulletproof glass. And what's in my mind immediately is that, oh, no. No, no, no. This barrel is freshly painted. There's people here with cameras and stuff. Please don't crap all over this barrel. That was in my mind. Meanwhile we're on a 25-second second countdown: 25, 24—

JEFF PETKOVICH

[UNINTELLIGIBLE]

PETER DEBERNARDI

Sounds in the barrel were, of course, the two-way communication we had with our crew. Our crew chief had the radio and he was telling us how many feet away we were from the brink. He was giving us a description of everything that was happening. And we had a stereo. That's a story itself. I'll tell you later on the story of how these fellows programmed the music.

Well, I can say it. My barrel partner, Jeff, he says, guy, we got to have tunes in there, you know? And he's just quite a fellow. He said, you got to have tunes in there. And the tunes were, believe it or not—the guys did a good job programming the tape. They should be music directors,

I swear, at a radio station. As soon as I hit the river, the first song was
"Riverboat Fantasy." Then the next song was "Dead or Alive" by Bon
Jovi. You know, after we go over. I mean, these guys, what a warped
sense of humor.

JEFF PETKOVICH

We're going down, Peter.

PETER DEBERNARDI

[BLEEP]

JEFF PETKOVICH

We're going down.

PETER DEBERNARDI

Now, prior to doing the falls, I always thought it'd be something like a
fast elevator ride—super fast. You know that feeling you get inside, real
queasy, like, woo. No, not at all. Not at all. And we did a 360 back flip,
and I didn't believe what I was looking at because it felt like you lied
down on the couch and went to bed, lying perfectly horizontal. And it
was peaceful. It was so peaceful. The serenity, even with the music—for
three and a half seconds.

After three and a half seconds, though, we hit, yes, that rock that was the
size of a house. Hit the side of that. Water blew in at the same time. Then
we went under the surface, hit two more times. And I can remember it
shifted the barrel. It twisted it like a 180 in a circle. I remember we hit
two more times. Everything went kind of translucent, white, darkest
color. Then, of course, we hit two more times, then it surfaced. And then
it was all over.

I remember Jeff yelling out, we did it. We did it. There were a few
profanities here and there, which I won't say right now.

JEFF PETKOVICH

Woo-hoo! Woo! We're OK! [BLEEP] right we're OK! Peter, what a [BLEEP]
buzz, eh?

PETER DEBERNARDI

We [BLEEP] made it, man.

JEFF PETKOVICH

Put her there, bud!

PETER DEBERNARDI

But when we came out of the barrel, I can tell you, we were able to climb out of that thing right at the base of the falls, right at the bottom of Table Rock, the lower observation deck. And I tell you, because you're so sealed in that thing, when those hatches were opened up, that was a nice vision, seeing the crew chief's face sticking in the hatch and it was opened up. And what a feeling when you climb out of that thing. And, of course, people are applauding all around, and the crew's got big smiles on their faces. And you're literally looking straight up—we were that close to the base—at what you had just done and went over that magnificent beauty.

After the stunt, I had never went down there. Six years, seven years. I live no more than a half a mile from it too. That's ironic about this, that it's hard for me to believe that I've done that, bottom line. It seems like a dream, like that wasn't me that went over. It was somebody else.

You know, to this day, though, I don't try to act like a smart ass, like, yeah, we did the falls. Yeah, wow, super stunt men here. No. Not at all. I have the admiration that, thank you for letting it happen, because it let us through. Whatever forces there were, whatever happened, I was allowed to do that. And she let me do it.

Credits.

APPOGGIATURA

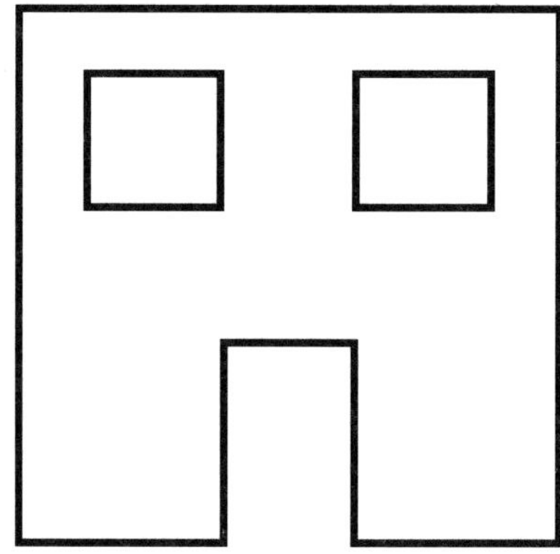

It's a simple test. In fact, it could barely be called a test. You are asked to do nothing consciously. You sit in the chin rest, forehead pressed against the guard, and allow your eyes to peer into the lens to focus on the image in front of you. The lights are dim and dramatic, the room is quiet and strange, and the machines feel just one lightning shock away from taking on lives of their own. But as you concentrate on the image, all of these things recede and leave you with nothing but the picture of a barn centralized on a green lawn, with a fence-lined road leading from the barn door directly out of the center of the frame. Slowly, the borders of each crisp boundary lose their edge, atomizing slightly—green diffusing into blue, red diffusing into green, confusing the eye. Yet as soon as the image has been given license to bleed, it is scolded, told to reform itself, and stand at attention with proper boundaries. Immediately, the image returns, clear as the day it represents.

This repeats a few times before the next test begins, perhaps followed by the familiar letter chart, or the more aggressive pressure test, measuring the resistance of your eyeball. Yet none of the tests are as unique or uncanny as what I'll call "the blurring home test." Only here does one witness the completely unconscious activity of "zoning out," of losing focus, daydreaming or drifting—along with the sudden shock of returning to what remains incontrovertibly present—like when reading a book and realizing that the word has pushed one past the literal page and the words go fuzzy without one's realizing it. The book becomes secondary; everything around you becomes secondary. In that moment, the mind wanders through different virtual passages, unearthing what the book held like a bizarre catalyst and activating a maze of thoughts until perhaps there is a blip. The interruption could be as simple as a sunbeam shifting over the course of time, finally reaching one's eyes and disrupting the virtual haze, blinking the actual book back into one's primary frame. These moments hypnotically drive a person into strange arenas that don't have any clear geometrical markings but nevertheless remain latent within Cartesian space, awaiting agitation to emerge.

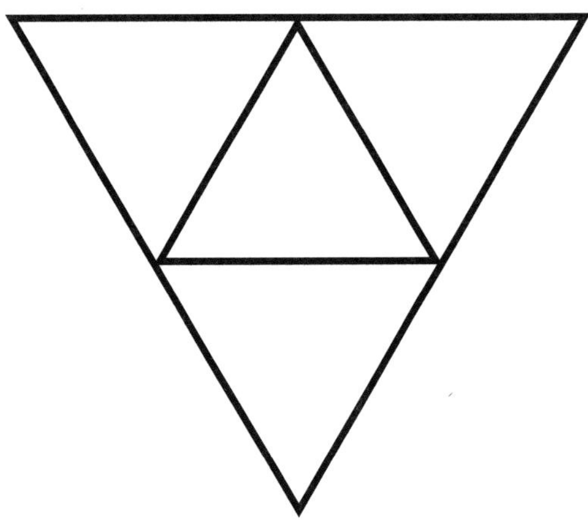

This emergence insists on the power that things have in and over our lives. The banalities, oddities, or necessities that occupy space also make it possible to leave that space altogether. Objects all hold the endless capacity to estrange us from the comfort of the given; to evoke what remains unseen, or previously unthought. An object can do this on its own, but it can also do it as a series working together. There is, of course, the exhibition, and then there are the artworks that make up the exhibition. The exhibition does not exist without the artworks; nevertheless, an artwork on its own does not make the same exhibition. It is like divorcing an organ from the body. There is an autonomy to this organ as flesh, but a particular set of its functions are contingent upon being in a body, functioning together with other organs, receiving blood and doing its part in the constant upkeep of living. The artwork is, in a sense, an object within a larger object, just like a person can exist on his or her own, but when a mass of people begin to form, a different mentality emerges altogether. The movement, the feeling, and the ardor of the mass sings a different song from the single person. The mass can envelop you; the person can face you. The song can wash over you; the note can strike you. A room of begonias overwhelms you, a single display endears you. Each has its own particular cadence, resulting from the separateness of each, albeit with rather blurry borders.

One might focus on these borders to suggest that there is no object, only a convenient fiction of the mind. Close inquiry at the edge of an object reveals that its solidity is fabricated; that the object is instead a radical fraying: porous, trembling, a dynamic glut of flux. Implicit in this perspective is an effective atomization of the world, where one can always look closer and see that things are not what they seem. However, we do not find out how organs work based on their quantum jitters, nor do we understand a country's dynamics by looking at protons and neutrons. To reduce objects and phenomena to a final substrate narrows our reality so that meaning is lost. Rather, one should preserve objecthood at all levels of scale to understand the power of each register.

Implied in this atomization is the belief that the world is governed by forces existent before matter has anything to say. Therefore non-material forces engender all the world's complexity, giving life to matter. This, however, would get us into the tricky divide between dead and living matter. Rather than trying to find a complicated solution, let's embrace the simplest. Instead of force begetting object, object begets force. Thus, there is no magnetic field without a conductive metal, no gravity without a mass, no violence without warring fronts. There is no range of forces, no range of meanings without the object. One might look to the color theory of Matisse for a strange but welcome fellow traveler. Matisse knew that a red patch is a far cry from a red banner, that a red rooibos stain remains merely polite in comparison to red oil paint slathered on canvas.[1] It might be then assumed that the force of an object is entirely based on its relations: no inherent force of the object without light, without a spectator, without someone comparing and contrasting. Certainly no object exists within a vacuum, but no object can be fully revealed in its relations. No amount of probing or prying, copying or recreating will exhaust the object. It always has some hidden reserve. Without such a reserve, the relations between objects could not continue to surprise. We are on occasion held in a trance by such a selection of things. For sometimes objects conspire to expand and contract space and vision, doing so by relying on both the apparent features of each individual object, and the more transcendent features of the experience of the whole.

1.   Yve-Alain Bois, "Matisse and 'Arche-drawing,'"
     in *Painting as Model* (Cambridge:
     MIT Press, 1993).

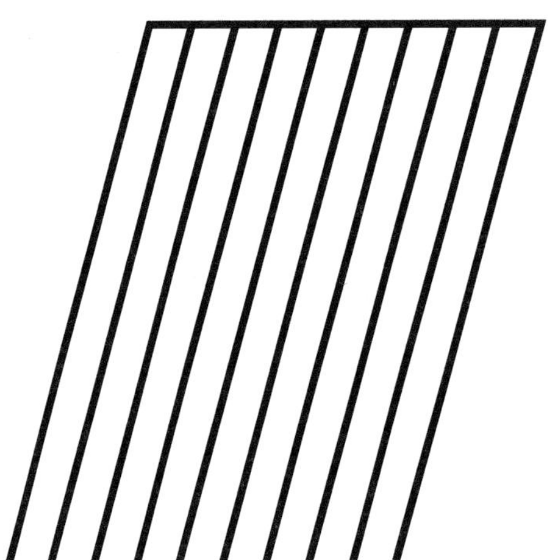

The transcendent, in this case, is not religious or spiritual. As means to clarify the term, we might look to the phenomena of light streaming through the clouds, known as Jacob's ladder. First described in the Book of Genesis, Jacob lay down to rest and dreamt of a ladder that reached the heavens where angels and God could ascend and descend, uniting earth and heaven into one domain. God speaks his prophecy to Jacob and, upon hearing it, Jacob wakes, understanding the dream as a sign that the land where he lay was indeed God's land—the veritable gates of heaven.

These Judeo-Christian overtones linger over the empirical phenomena, and certainly, many still look at these rays of light as quietly singing the Lord's name. But I think that this event is just as wondrous viewed simply as material phenomenon. These rays of light become substantial not because of any omniscient mediator, but because of a material mediation. When light falls on a blue cup it awakens its particular mottled shades of blue. Light becomes visible when it hits matter that can make it so—whether that be vapor after a brief rain, dust from a just-beaten rug, or pollution from a new industrial complex. Light has its wave and particle duality, but without something to bounce off of, the phenomena remains invisible to our eyes. In the instance of dust, rather than seeing the surface of the blue cup or a thing simply reflecting light, dust allows us to see the approximate shape of light itself. Light does not miraculously become sculptural. It converses with particles in the air, creating an effect that remains wondrous regardless of any explanation. The appearance of light as a nearly tangible object reveals the tiny and neglected bits of the world and how they play their roles without our noticing. Dust is our way of interacting with this invisible object.

This evocation of the invisible suggests that all the spaces we might see as empty are filled with things and materials of all kinds, able to perhaps quietly change our movements, perceptions and thoughts. Spaces have their own lives, and we constantly participate in them regardless of our awareness. Instead, we naturalize space to make it a neutral backdrop for our lives, intentions, and emotions. A good thought experiment, then, would be to imagine all of one's familiar spaces filled with water. Imagine that we could breathe in this strange new underwater world, and wade through the water's resistance, noting the rippled, bluish light that webs across all surfaces, realigning all nearby phenomena and revealing the implicit experiential contingency of any space. Every common quality will have changed, each appearing in a whole new way as everything sways in and out of focus, everything further away because of the work required to move. Any movement we ourselves make creates waves, affecting nearby objects. Likewise, we can detect the movements of other objects, if range allows. And lastly, any object placed inside or removed outside this tank of water-filled space would displace its corresponding volume, negatively or positively. If there are too many things in the room, the space will overflow. Finding the right tension means finding the right number of objects to put in a room. Any addition or subtraction of objects, any change in architecture, or a tweak in the lighting, any movement of an object changes the pressure of a space.

The density of air is a feature we have become accustomed to, removing it from the equations of our interactions. Increasing this density foregrounds the implicit relationships of movement and pressure while also retuning our sensibilities to what we prosaically call "negative" and"positive" space. The unseen may not be negative but only a different kind of density of space, distant on the register of the material spectrum ranging from gas to solid. Thus, as a body moving through space, we are not walking through emptiness, encountering positive forms along the way, but wading through air, dust, and other invisible actors, some perhaps suggesting the age of a space or traces of things that were recently there.

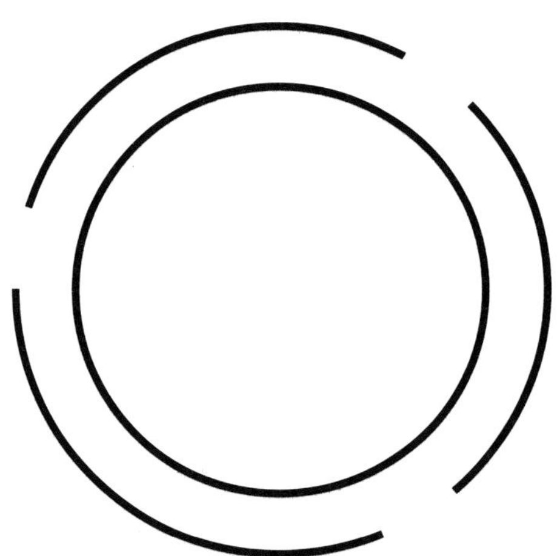

In the heart of Harvard, in a chamber that was noted to be completely and absolutely anechoic, sat an eager John Cage, awaiting the experience of absolute silence. Instead, he discovered that there was no such thing. In a room of total isolation, Cage realized that as long as he had a beating heart, a pulsing brain, and breath left in his lungs, there would be no such thing as silence. Each would provide a set of rhythms, blips, and rumbles. Cage's seminal piece *4'33"* is a result of this realization and is a similar experiment to our water tank. The piece is formally very simple. The performer comes to a piano, reveals the keys, and rests for four minutes and thirty-three seconds. The gesture, however, is more complicated. Cage concisely foregrounds context—the givens of an environment, the expectations of an audience—and makes the performance out of what is normally considered the negative, elucidating two crucial ideas: absolute silence is a fiction, and relative silence isn't negative as much as it is the active partner of sound. Music, in its most simplistic form, was not based on melody, harmony, or pitch, but the moments between noise and rest, or in other words—rhythm.

Cage's techniques for composition, such as using the I Ching to determine notation, unfortunately hid the apparent structures of the resulting rhythms, and could not be easily sensed by a listener. Some composers who came after him desired something more transparent. New York–based composer Steve Reich wanted a "compositional process and a sounding music that [were] one in the same thing." This, however, prompted a friend to say that this would demystify the music, leaving no surprises for the listener. Reich responds:

> The use of hidden structural devices in music never appealed to me. Even when all the cards are on the table and everyone hears what is gradually happening in a musical process there are still enough mysteries to satisfy all. These mysteries are the impersonal, unintended, psychoacoustic by-products of the intended process. These might include submelodies heard within repeated melodic patterns, stereophonic effects due to listener location, slight irregularities in performance, harmonics, difference tones, etc.

Listening to an extremely gradual musical process opens my ears to it, but it always extends farther than I can hear, and that makes it interesting to listen to that musical process again. That area of every gradual (completely controlled) musical process, where one hears the details of the sound moving out away from intentions, occurring for their own acoustic reasons, is it.[2]

Reich's two paragraphs read as a minor manifesto that hailed an entire era of a minimalist mindset. This acknowledgment of a new way to deal with time, process, and repetition demonstrate the obvious overlap between music and visual structure. Within the visual arts, repetition is one of the key resources with which to develop rhythms. The number of repetitions, the size of each object, the difference between each repetition as a way to create development, time, narrative, and shifts within color, texture, size, shape, and idea, each and every displacement affect the larger object: the exhibition as a whole. Color, shape, line, texture, and material—the very basic constituents of visual language—all play a central role to the visual composition that emerges through space and time, and even if there is no mystery in each individual creation, there are unintended visual echoes, overtones, and harmonics that enact a visual performance capable of affecting even the most skeptical viewer.

An exhibition is often the result of an artist responding to the givens of a setting. It's a form of composition that regards the already present forces and feelings of a space and further negotiates what one can do with them. How can one enhance its rhythms? How can one cajole and organize the pressure points? How can one create a composition of flows and stoppages, rests and noise?

2. Steve Reich, *Writings on Music, 1965-2000* (New York: Oxford University Press, 2002).

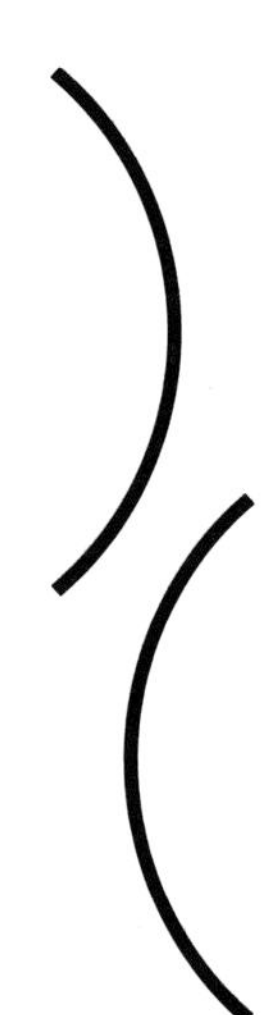

All objects displace space upon their introduction, but many objects won't sit still even when they find their place. They continue to move and jerk about, creating waves and pressures by themselves. Consider a set of contact lenses—the fruit of one's previous labor at the optometrist's office—swimming in saline solution. On occasion, they flip inside out within their case. All they need, really, is a slight touch, and they will spasm back and forth, between convex and concave. To change their curvature and their appearance, a lens need not change its material. All that's needed is a flip, where the object materially stays the same, but its capacities and forces are rearranged; where it doesn't displace liquid, but pushes it, forces it to occupy space differently.

The flip between convex and concave marks the force generated by the object. This simple mechanism or spasm might be the final corrective measure needed to see things as they are. Silence and noise are not so far apart, but the force generated by the gap between them certainly resonates. Positive and negative space must not be thought of as radically separate, but of the same material existing at different densities. When these densities are allowed to mingle, one can feel the weather of a space more distinctly. With a completely homogenous pressure, we would notice very little. It takes agitation to cause us to sense the atmosphere. Only then are we able to notice the things we inhabit, the things that inhabit us, and the things that often remain unseen.

* * *

High above us are two cosmic eyes, peering over our planet in turns. As the sun sets, we see the eye of the moon begin to open, and as awake as the sun's shadow will allow. The waxing and waning of the moon, its shift from convex to concave, enables us to see the power of things on a much larger scale. The moon's gravitational pull directly affects the waters of our planet, creating the tides and the constant shifts in oceans. The liquid-filled room is no longer the space of the exhibition, but interplanetary space, where the objects within literally create waves based on their orientations and movements. Gravity is not a force that exists before the object. It is one immanent to the object, and it is one of many. Objects exert themselves, interact with one another and subtly or excessively rearrange time and space, ideas and concepts, the physical and the immaterial. They resonate for all those that are able to hear.

Ajay Kurian for Jacob Kassay

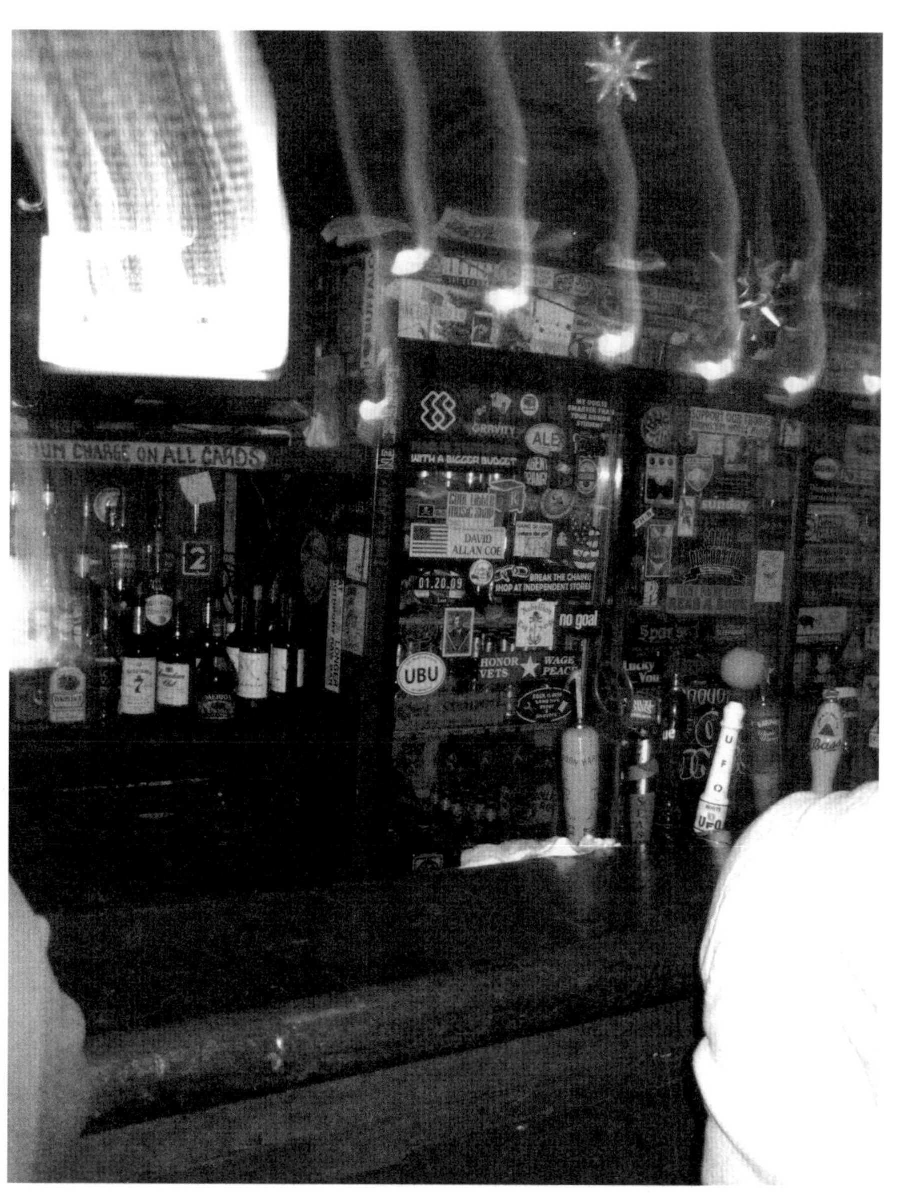

Credits

The Power Station is a not-for-profit initiative dedicated to providing a platform for ambitious contemporary art projects in Dallas, Texas. Housed in a Power & Light building constructed in 1920, artists are invited to respond to the raw character of the architecture, offering an alternative to the traditional gallery and museum context.

Geared toward an international audience and most immediately, the community of Dallas, the bold programming serves as a catalyst to provocate public discourse around art and culture.

Projects and publications at The Power Station are made possible through funding provided by The Pinnell Foundation.

The Power Station would like to thank the following people for their contributions to the exhibition *No Goal*: A special thank you to Matt Kantar for his assistance during the installation, Rob Teeters, Michael Capio, Danielle Avram Morgan, Bob Sullivan, David Hocker, Janelle Pinnell, Hilyer Santizo, Benjamin Godsill, Kevin Todora, Catherine MacMahon, Jesse Francis and Matt Morgan.

Design: Front Desk Apparatus
Editing: Rachel Bohan
Printed and Bound by: Cassochrome, Belgium
Edition: 1,000

Published by The Power Station

The Power Station
3816 Commerce Street
Dallas, TX 75226
www.powerstationdallas.com

Published on the occasion of the exhibition
No Goal held at The Power Station, Dallas
April 11– July 13, 2012

ISBN: 978-0-9840230-3-5

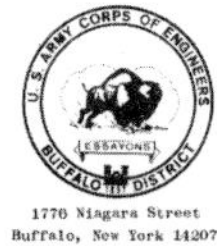